(214) 374-2485

INTERVIEWS THAT WORK

SECOND EDITION

Interviews That Work

A Practical Guide for Journalists

Shirley Biagi
California State University, Sacramento

Wadsworth Publishing Company
Belmont, California
A Division of Wadsworth, Inc.

Communication Editor: Kristine Clerkin
Editorial Assistant: Nancy Spellman
Production Editor: Donna L. Linden
Designer: Kaelin Chappell
Print Buyer: Barbara Britton
Permissions Editor: Robert Kauser
Copy Editor: Robert Fiske
Compositor: Weimer Typesetting, Indianapolis, Indiana
Cover Illustration: Francis Livingston
Printer: Maple Press

This book is printed on acid-free paper that meets Environmental Protection Agency standards for recycled paper.

2 3 4 5 6 7 8 9 10—96 95 94 93 92

Library of Congress Cataloging-in-Publication Data

Biagi, Shirley.
    Interviews that work : a practical guide for journalists / Shirley
Biagi. —2nd ed.
        p.   cm.
    Includes bibliographical references and index.
    ISBN 0-534-15966-4
    1. Interviewing in Journalism.   I. Title.
PN4784.I6B53   1992
070.4'3—dc20   91-9000

■ CONTENTS

■ PREFACE

To gather the information for the first edition of this book, I traveled nearly 40,000 miles throughout the United States and Canada to interview 45 print and broadcast reporters and other experts on the art and craft of interviewing.

In a sense, some of the people chose themselves. By having the jobs they do, network television reporters are visible, and we see how they work every day.

Some of the journalists I knew already. I had seen their work, and I admired what they do. Some of the journalists had won awards. But the majority of the journalists I interviewed were chosen by their colleagues, as reporters whose interviewing skills are exceptional.

For the second edition of *Interviews That Work*, I've added some new case study examples (but some were just too good to give up). The new case studies include examples from Linda Gomez of *Life* magazine covering the drug trade in Mexico and from George Curry of the *Chicago Tribune*, interviewing the controversial leader of the Nation of Islam, Louis Farrakhan. Maryln Schwartz of the *Dallas Morning News* and John Martin of ABC News also have added new interviewing case study experiences.

And since the first edition, I've spoken to many professional journalism organizations, including the American Press Institute, the Association for Education in Journalism and Mass Communication, the Society of Professional Journalists, and the Poynter Institute for Media Studies. One of the questions I always ask is: "What did I forget to cover in my book?"

As a result of these comments, I've added suggestions about how to interview children in Chapter 6. I've also added a public relations case study in Chapter 11. I hope these changes will make this edition of *Interviews That Work* even more useful.

When I began this project in 1985, as an interviewer interviewing expert interviewers about interviewing, I worried about my technique. Shouldn't I be the consummate interviewer—the one whose interviews are completely unflawed? I quickly gave up that idea at my first interview in Washington, D.C., when my tape cassette catapulted itself out of the tape recorder into the lap of my interviewee.

Then I arrived in Florida with a summer cold, and I survived the interviews by sneezing through three boxes of tissue and drinking a dozen cups of hot tea with lemon. When I listened to the tapes of the interviews later, I sounded as though I were talking from inside a fish tank.

In Honolulu, I invited an interviewee to talk with me at lunch. She told me she was surprised. She said she never does interviews while she eats because she can't eat and talk at the same time. She didn't know how hungry I was.

Some of the other interviewees were just as helpful. One journalist watched my tape recorder for me and told me when it was time to turn over the cassette. Another grabbed my tape recorder, took out the tape, and slapped the cassette on the table when the tape stopped working. The tape worked perfectly after that.

Like all interviewers, I'm always learning how to improve what I do. As I progressed through my list of interviewees, I tested the strategies these reporters suggested, and my last interview was a triumph compared to my first.

Listen to what these journalists can teach you about how they do research, how they take notes, how they get answers to their questions, and how they write their stories. You will learn that, as one journalist told me, "Interviewing is a skill that only improves through knowledge and experience. You can't get worse at it. You can only get better."

■ ACKNOWLEDGMENTS

Grateful thanks to all the journalists and scholars who spent time talking with me.

Dean Bacquet, formerly a Reporter for *The Times-Picayune* (New Orleans, La.) and the *Chicago Tribune*; now a Reporter for *The New York Times*.

Gary Bannerman, Host of "Bannerline," a news interview program in Chilliwack, Canada. Also writes a column for *North Shore News*, a tri-weekly paper in Vancouver, B.C.

John Berthelson, Reporter, *The Asian Wall Street Journal*, Bangkok, Thailand.

Daphne Bramham, formerly a Reporter for Canadian Press Wire Service; now a Reporter for *The Vancouver Sun*.

David Brinkley, Host, "This Week with David Brinkley," ABC News, Washington, D.C.

Joel Brinkley, Jerusalem Bureau Chief, *The New York Times*.

Fred Chafe, retired as Chief of Bureau, Canadian Press Wire Service.

Roy Peter Clark, Dean of the Faculty, Poynter Institute for Media Studies.

Beverly Creamer, Reporter, *The Honolulu Advertiser*.

George E. Curry, New York Bureau Chief, *Chicago Tribune*.

Stuart Dim, Director of News Service, University of Medicine and Dentistry of New Jersey.

Sam Donaldson, former Chief White House Correspondent, ABC News; now Co-anchor of "Primetime Live," ABC.

Douglas Dowie, former Managing Editor, *Daily News* (Los Angeles).

William Endicott, formerly Capitol Bureau Chief, *Los Angeles Times*; now Capitol Bureau Chief, *The Sacramento Bee.*

Joseph T. Francke, former Legal Counsel, California Newspaper Publishers Association; now Executive Director, California First Amendment Coalition.

Kristin Gilger, Assistant to the Editor, *The Times-Picayune* (New Orleans, La.).

Linda Gomez, Reporter, *Life* magazine.

Marlane Guelden, formerly a Reporter for *The Davis* (Calif.) *Enterprise*; now a Freelance Writer and Photographer in Bangkok, Thailand.

Seymour Hersh, formerly a Reporter for *The New York Times*; author of *The Target Is Destroyed: What Really Happened to Flight 007 and What America Knew About It.*

David Hudson, Chair, Speech Department, Golden West College, Huntington Beach.

Salim Jiwa, Reporter, *The Province,* Vancouver, B.C.

Brian Kennedy, Reporter, Broadcast News, Vancouver, B.C.

Bonnie Raines Kettner, Assistant Editor, *The Province,* Vancouver, B.C.

Virginia Kidd, Professor, Department of Communication, California State University, Sacramento.

Ted Koppel, Anchorman, "Nightline," ABC News.

June Kronholz, formerly a Reporter for *The Wall Street Journal*; resigned in August 1989; now living in Australia.

Laurier LaPierre, former Host of "Laurier's People," CKVU-TV, Vancouver, B.C.; producer of 13-part program on CBUT-TV, "Beyond the Line."

Paula LaRocque, Assistant Managing Editor, *The Dallas Morning News.*

Gerald Lanson, Assistant City Editor, *San Jose Mercury News.*

Matt Levi, formerly a Reporter for KGMB-TV, Honolulu.

John Martin, National Correspondent, ABC News, Washington, D.C.

Frank McCulloch, Managing Editor, *Examiner* (San Francisco).

Tommy Miller, Assistant Managing Editor, *Houston Chronicle.*

Bill Nottingham, formerly a Business Writer for *St. Petersburg Times*; now Assistant City Editor, *Los Angeles Times*, Orange County edition.

Bob Osterberg, Station Manager, KDES-AM, Palm Springs.

Walt Philbin, Police Reporter, *The Times-Picayune* (New Orleans, La.).

Peter Rinearson, Reporter, *The Seattle Times.*

Maryln Schwartz, Columnist, *The Dallas Morning News.*

Bill Stall, Editorial Writer, *Los Angeles Times.*

Susan Stamberg, former Co-host of "All Things Considered," National Public Radio.

Leigh Stephens, Professor, Department of Journalism, California State University, Sacramento.

Teresa Stepzinski, formerly a Reporter for *The Beaumont Enterprise*; now a Reporter for the *Florida Times-Union*.

Doug Swanson, Reporter, *The Dallas Morning News*, New York bureau.

Sandra Thompson, Assistant Managing Editor—News Features, *St. Petersburg Times.*

Reviewers

Special gratitude to the second edition reviewers, who offered many good suggestions.

Charles Adair, SUNY—Buffalo
Pat Cranston, University of Washington
Edward H. Sewell, Jr., Virginia Polytechnic Institute and State University

Thanks again to the first edition reviewers, who offered encouragement and good advice.

James Bow, Kent State University
Charles Burke, University of Florida
William E. Hall, Ohio State University
Barbara W. Hartung, San Diego State University
Dennis R. Jones, University of Southern Mississippi
Donald A. Lambert, Ohio University
John Luter, University of Hawaii
James A. Wollert, Memphis State University

Thanks also to Donna Willman, VU/TEXT and to Jan Haag.

CREDITS

INTERVIEWS THAT WORK

1

Why You Should Become a Good Interviewer

A giant clock ticks every day over the imperfect process of reporting. Working under the ogre of deadlines, reporters always hope to find an interviewee with a quick quote to give insight, a perceptive quote to explain, a poignant quote to add empathy.

Informative, entertaining stories originate from well-organized, well-conducted interviews. Readers and viewers rarely realize how many interviews, how much research, how much time reporters invest in each story. But all newspaper and broadcast stories result from various forms of questioning—a two-minute telephone call to the Chamber of Commerce to find out the average price of a home, a 20-minute cab ride with a presidential candidate on the way to the airport, or a five-hour discussion with a convicted murderer.

"You have to think of journalism as a service industry, somewhat like the milkman, or what used to be the milkman," says David Brinkley. "I mean, everybody could keep his own cow, but it's more convenient to buy milk. They could go to the Soviet Union, theoretically, but it's more convenient to let us do it for them."

How important is the skill of interviewing to a reporter?

- "Fundamental."—Ted Koppel, ABC News

- "Critical. There are no star reporters in America who are not good interviewers. If you don't acquire a skillful technique, you're going to be in trouble from your first day as a reporter."—Joel Brinkley, *The New York Times*

- ■ "Skillful interviewing is the basis for all good reporting and writing."—Kristin Gilger, *The* (New Orleans) *Times-Picayune*
- ■ "If you don't get the information, you don't have the story."—George Curry, *Chicago Tribune*

What You'll Find in This Book

Good interviewing demands intellect, patience, empathy, perseverance and wit. Learning to become a better interviewer is like learning to become a better writer. "You can't make somebody a better writer, but you can show someone what good writers do," says Joel Brinkley. "You can't teach somebody how to interview, but you can show someone what good interviewers do."

Yet journalists rarely get a chance to peek in on their colleagues' interviews. Reporters watch other reporters work only in group interviews (at a press conference or when two reporters team up to interview one person) or in broadcast interviews that show the questions and the answers. Many reporters know very little about the questioning techniques their colleagues use.

This book offers a chance to sit behind a two-way mirror and observe what recognized journalists do to make their interviews work. You will be there, learning from their successes as well as their frustrations.

You also will hear many different kinds of reporters talk about many different types of interviews—from a broadcast reporter in Vancouver to a Washington, D.C., correspondent for a major newspaper; from the chief of a small newspaper bureau near New Orleans to a television network correspondent. Through this book, these people will talk to you and with you about the skills every reporter must master. You'll also learn from their mistakes.

"I'm never really pleased a hundred percent with what I do," says Bill Nottingham. "I have to call people back to ask them how to spell their names. I'm capable of making the foolish errors as easily as somebody just out of journalism school."

Kristin Gilger says, "Most reporters, I believe, are competent enough interviewers to get a story. The problem is missing information, either because the reporter has already made up his mind about what he wants from the interview and closes the interview before the person has had his say or because the reporter lacks the compassion and curiosity to get more than the facts—the description, the details, the 'why' of the story."

Introspective reporters like Nottingham and Gilger realize that reporters are continually frustrated by the limits of time. The ideal situation is to have weeks for research before an interview and weeks to write the story afterward. But this is a fantasy. Reporters usually write an interview story the day they do the interview.

"My role," says Sam Donaldson, "is to find out what's really going on . . . . I usually fail. Usually I don't have the ability, the facility, the access, and sometimes, the intelligence to really see what's going on. But that's the goal every day. I make the attempt."

Types of Interview Stories

Before you decide whom you should interview for a story, you must know what kind of story you're writing. You have several choices: a news story, a news feature, a profile, an investigative story or a round-up.

News Story

News means change. An event that happens with impact and importance for your community today will be reported as news. Typically, a news story reports the traditional who, what, why, where, when and sometimes how an event occurred. For Kristin Gilger, the story was a confrontation with a gun between a husband and wife: "Fourth-graders at LaPlace school watched in stunned silence Friday afternoon as their teacher rushed outside and scuffled with his gun-wielding wife. One shot was fired during the fight between Adrian Claudet and his wife, Joyce, but neither was wounded, St. John the Baptist Parish [county] authorities said."

Gilger found a witness to the shooting. In a telephone interview, the witness (a teacher in the classroom next to Adrian Claudet) said, "I just figured whatever was going on out there did not concern me or the children in that classroom. I shut the door and told the children to take their seats and continue with their math homework."

News Feature

A news feature can carefully examine the how or why in a news story or give background details about the who or what. A news feature can run alongside a news story as a sidebar to explain some aspect of the news event, or a news feature can be a follow-up to a news story. The *Los Angeles Times* published a news feature interview with John G. McMillian a week after McMillian's underdog company, Northwest Pipeline Corporation, won the contract to build the Alaska pipeline.

Reporter Bill Stall flew from Los Angeles to McMillian's home in Salt Lake City, Utah, and Stall and McMillian sat on the front porch for three hours and talked. Stall says the relaxed, unintimidating location made McMillian particularly candid. McMillian said, "You've got to realize there were 16 companies in there including Exxon and Royal Dutch Shell and Gulf of Canada. And these are a bunch of arrogant bastards. I mean Exxon only talks to God on the days they want to."

Profile

The goal of a profile is to focus on one person by painting a word or a video portrait. If the person is familiar to your readers, you want to teach them something new. If the person is an unknown, you must completely sketch the person's character. Sometimes what a person does is more important than what a person says.

In Amritsar, India, reporter June Kronholz interviewed Jarnail Singh Bhindranwale, a Sikh fundamentalist. The "sant" (priest) Bhindranwale was accused of directing murder squads in India. "He was taking refuge in the Holy Temple," says Kronholz, "surrounded by his spear-carrying followers, preaching his lessons of hatred and terror.

"As was the custom for anyone entering the temple, I wore a covering on my head—in this case, a borrowed dish towel—and was shoeless. He wore an orange turban, a long scraggly beard, a blue tunic and a pistol in a holster.

"He was reclining on a charpoy, a string bed. His men lined the room, each carrying a spear or long rifle; other men reclined on string beds surrounding his. The sant used the interview to entertain his followers with derisory comments about foreigners, and so had nothing of substance to say to me.

"Still, the interview was far from a failure. There are some interviews you do because you want answers. There are others where you know the answers and instead want color, atmosphere, mood and a good quote. Bhindranwale, wanted for murder, holed up in a temple, spinning his pistol on his finger, entertaining his fanatic followers with insults, made a terrific interview, even if he said nothing."

Investigative Story

An investigative story answers how and why more relentlessly than a simple news story that answers what. The story exists because a reporter chooses to take the time and energy to investigate beyond what is generally known about an event. An investigative story belongs to the reporter exclusively before it belongs to the reader. The reporter generates the story from information, tips, research and interviews.

Bonnie Raines Kettner was covering government in Victoria, Vancouver's capital, when she learned that the government in British Columbia planned to cut doctor's wages. In a front-page story, Kettner wrote:

> The B.C. [British Columbia] government will ask provincial doctors to take a voluntary cut in fees, *The Province* has learned.
>
> And if they don't co-operate, the government will consider forcibly rolling back the 14-per-cent hike that came into effect in April as part of the doctors' two-year contract with the government, sources say.
>
> Such a move would mean breaking an existing contract.
>
> Rollbacks of previously-negotiated wage hikes for doctors and health professionals are one of a number of money-saving options in the government's $2-billion health budget being considered as part of the restraint drive, sources say. . . .

Round-Up

This symposium-style story gives a reader perspective on a current issue by gathering together several people's opinions. A writer can report a round-up of opinion or a round-up of comments on one specific topic.

Maryln Schwartz decided to use this story approach to tell her readers what rich North Dallas women gave their hairdressers for Christmas. Schwartz wrote:

> Rosemary Everett has her priorities with Christmas presents. She's giving her mother a crockpot. She's giving her hairdresser an all-expenses-paid trip to Mexico City. "Well, let's face it," says the North Dallas woman. "My mother doesn't come out to my house in the middle of a rainstorm to do my hair for an important party. And my hairdresser wouldn't either if I didn't make it worth his while. Besides, my mother will be perfectly satisfied with a crockpot. My hairdresser won't. . . ."
>
> "You bet I give my hairdresser good tips and impressive gifts," says Angela Martin, who is married to a Richardson oil-man. "One year, I decided to economize and give him after-shave lotion. Soon after, I showed up at a big charity ball and had the same hairdo as 10 of his other customers. But the woman who gave him a videotape recorder had the most exquisite hairdo I've ever seen. . . ."

Arellia Gray, a Highland Park divorcee who's been giving her hairdresser extravagant gifts for the past 20 years, says the whole idea isn't as excessive as it sounds.

"Look, we can afford to give stereo systems and suits from Nei-man-Marcus. But we expect something in return. I spend up to $400 a month at the hairdresser's. Bored, rich women can be very trying. Believe me, the hairdressers earn every penny of those $500 and $600 Christmas gifts. And besides, the shops are just so much fun at the holidays. There's always champagne and food overflowing at all the best ones. You just can't help but get into the spirit of things."

What Is an Interview?

The goal of all reporters is to collect complete, accurate, fair information. A good interviewer looks for a revelation or an insight, a thought or a viewpoint that is interesting, worth listening to, not commonly heard and not already known.

Like a conversation, an interview is an exchange of information, opinion or experience from one person to another. In a conversation, control of the discussion passes back and forth from one person to the other. In an interview, however, the interviewer causes the discussion to happen and determines the direction of the questioning.

"An interview is not a conversation," says Sandra Thompson. "You really have to squelch your ego totally while at the same time maintaining a completely hidden control. That's hard. I don't think people realize how hard it is.

"You're monitoring everything that's said while creating a casual, relaxed, non-threatening atmosphere. In reality, there's a tickertape going across the interviewer's mind—what must I ask again, what hand gestures is the person using, what is the person's tone of voice?"

An interviewer must simultaneously listen, observe, inquire, respond and record. "Sometimes I'm an interrogator, sometimes I'm a gadfly," says Ted Koppel. "Sometimes I'm a clarifier, sometimes I'm the deliberate witless." How well you succeed as an interviewer will depend on your ability to perform this journalistic gymnastic act.

Types of Interviews

Interviews range from cordial to antagonistic because interviewees range from effusive to defensive, depending on the information the interviewer wants and the circumstance of the interview. If you want to know what rich women give their hairdressers for Christmas, you probably have an approachable interviewee, proud to tell you about her largess. If you want to know about the government's plans to roll back doctors' fees, you probably face a reluctant interviewee. If you want to know how a small entrepreneur beat Exxon and 15 other bidders for the Alaska pipeline project, the interviewee will be cordial, willing. If you want to know what an eyewitness saw in the classroom next door as she watched a colleague argue with his wife over a gun, you probably will have to coax the interviewee to talk.

All good reporters must know how to gauge the person and the situation. You must be able to sense what to do at a certain moment—when to be nice, when to be tough, when to be wide-eyed and when to be nasty.

"I can't ever get that relaxed," says Susan Stamberg. "I have to always keep in mind where I'm going, whether I'm getting the answers that I need to explain my point. I can never get that chummy. It has to be a professional conversation."

A Final Word

Susan Stamberg and her print and broadcast colleagues share their experiences and their knowledge in the next 10 chapters. If you report for broadcast, Chapter 8 details the special circumstances that face the broadcast interviewer. The rest of the chapters will help you learn how to:

- get organized
- do research
- take notes
- get the interview
- conduct yourself during an interview
- ask good questions
- interview for broadcast
- choose and use quotes
- write what people say
- understand important legal and ethical issues

Brian Kennedy sums up the importance of all these skills for a reporter: "The better interviewer gets the better story."

Linda Gomez
Life magazine

Linda Gomez graduated with a degree in journalism from the University of California, Berkeley. She then moved to New York City, where she worked for *Life* magazine for eight years before returning to California, where she now reports for *Life* from San Francisco.

Linda Gomez has reported throughout Latin America for *Life,* but this story was more challenging than most. For three weeks, she traveled throughout Mexico documenting the drug traffic. In Mexico City, she faced the challenge of working with another reporter to gather a description of Rafael Caro Quintero, who had been charged with participating in the murder of U.S. Drug Enforcement Administration agent Enrique "Kiki" Camarena. This is a good example of how a tenacious, experienced reporter can get a story in a situation where other reporters would give up.

"I got into cahoots with a journalist of interesting scruples who [knew] how to get to Caro Quintero. Quintero is in prison, and his prison cell is carpeted; it's got a VCR, large TV screen, stove, refrigerator and stereo.

"The warden is being paid off, probably to the tune of about a million dollars a year by Caro Quintero to allow him to live in the style to which he is accustomed, including having two or three kilos of cocaine for his private use. Everything works by bribes whether it be money or drugs.

"I find I cannot get in to see Mr. Quintero without compromising myself in a way I don't wish to be compromised. So this journalist goes in for me, and now we have the next step, which is getting someone else to do your work. And how do you debrief [that person] immediately when they come out? It was the first time I had conducted an elaborate debriefing.

"I was not interested in what Caro Quintero said. I wanted to know what Caro Quintero was wearing. What was the ground like? Tell me what's on the wall. What were the food and vegetables? There are cases and cases of them. What is he wearing? What color is his shirt? What about his jewelry? Oh, he says a lot of it has been stolen. Interesting.

"What's around him? How many bodyguards does he have? Did you see evidence of cocaine usage? No, all right. That was important to me. Outside, what are the games they're playing? How many people are there?

"This is a specific way of questioning someone so that you don't plant them with answers. And not even later, when the whole story came out, did anybody have a description that was quite as good as the one we came to. If the story is any good, it ended up that way simply from brute labor and ox-like research."

SPECIAL REPORT
Harvest of Death
Tracking Drugs through Mexico
By Linda Gomez

The crimson petals have fallen. This month the poppy harvest begins in the mountains of western Mexico, much of the work done by children. It takes delicate hands to slice the flower pods and scrape up the white opium gum. By June, after the crop has crossed the border as heroin, some 4,000 Americans will have overdosed on the drug. Mexico's $40 billion drug trade is the impoverished nation's single booming industry, raking in more sales than those other international consortiums Procter & Gamble, Eastman Kodak and Coca-Cola combined. . . .

Among the dozens of sources for this account of the drug world is an intelligence operative who spent two decades in Mexican law enforcement combating traffickers. Now working for the U.S., he cannot reveal his real name—he calls himself Osuna—or his whereabouts. Since taking up residence in the U.S., he has moved four times. Even so, three attempts

have been made on his life by traffickers and corrupt Mexican cops. Osuna, who maintains an escort of bodyguards, knows their methods. "They'll strip and blindfold you and hang you from your thumbs," he says. "They mix highly flammable glue with gunpowder, then stick it to your body and light it."

The 1985 torture and murder of U.S. Drug Enforcement Administration agent Enrique "Kiki" Camarena revealed the viciousness, nerve and power of the Mexican drug world. Since then, the situation has only worsened. . . .

With their cash and guns, traffickers have taken advantage of Mexico's hard times, making offers difficult to refuse. Peasants eking out a subsistence living growing corn and beans are tempted to turn over patches of land for pot or poppies. State cops stand to make far more than their $100 per month salaries if they jump to the other side of the law. One federal policeman quit and joined the U.S. DEA after 10 years on the job. "All I ever wanted to be was a cop," he says, "but I was seeing evil all around me. My chief threw so much money around I thought he was a millionaire. I was naive—he was a crook who worked for the traffickers and got paid with bags of cash. People like him are vampires. They are bleeding the people. What we have in Mexico now is an army of bloodsuckers. I had to get out for my self-respect." Corruption in the military can be equally blatant. On drug raids, soldiers have been known to strip houses of everything—furniture, TV sets, even toilet paper. Explains Osuna: "Planters must pay off the army. If not, officers wait until harvest time to destroy the crop or take and sell it."

Top positions in Mexico's Federal Judicial Police have proved so lucrative in trafficker payoffs that in the early 1980s they were bought for as much as $100,000. In 1986 a $5 million stash of a federal police chief was seized—not a sum saved on a $700 monthly salary.

For a while, traffickers virtually owned Guadalajara. Protected by law-enforcement agents, airplanes loaded with cocaine taxied directly to a special hangar at Guadalajara International Airport. Traffickers shared a private radio band with the Department of Federal Security, Mexico's CIA and DEA. (One chief of the DFS, who has since fled Mexico, sold law-enforcement IDs at $100,000 each to traffickers.) Officials sometimes preferred to be paid in top-quality cocaine—to sell or snort themselves.

When these practices came to light during the investigation into the Camarena murder, they were sharply curtailed. Says Mexico's Attorney General Sergio Garcia Ramirez, "We're making a superhuman effort to stop the traffickers. Over 25,000 members of the army and 1,500 from my office are in the campaign." But his deputy adds, "Corruption just goes with drugs—speaking Spanish, English, whatever language it needs." U.S. and Mexican sources estimate that 70 percent of the federal agents in Mexico use cocaine. . . .

Rafael Caro Quintero, one of those indicted for the murder of Camarena, has remarkable amenities in his Mexico City prison. His cell is carpeted and equipped with a kitchen and VCR. He is allowed conjugal guests, and every Monday is sent cases of fresh fruits and vegetables, steaks, chops and Pepsi Cola. A spot inspection turned up 12 kilos (26 pounds) of cocaine in Caro Quintero's cushy quarters. (He said it was for his personal consumption.) Jailhouse drugs, some of them smuggled in in tamponlike containers by women visitors, also are used as bribes. Caro Quintero's minions even burrowed a 267-meter tunnel beneath the jail this winter, hoping to spring him. Authorities sealed it off before he could escape.

"Cops don't get wages from traffickers," Osuna notes. "They make it seem more like friendship. They use cocaine together, then the cops start receiving cash, cars, gold flasks, guns and ammo."

Contraband is transported from the primitive world of growers to the modern one of processors and consumers by burros, on humans, in fleets of tanker trucks and aboard aircraft that fly as low as 1,000 feet to evade radar. At least 2,500 unauthorized airstrips scar the Mexican landscape, from the Yucatan to the Rio Grande. Agents estimate that about 5,000 planes are involved in the Mexican traffickers' air force.

Cocaine destined for the U.S. originates in Colombia, Peru or Bolivia and is routed through Mexico. It is packed in army sacks called *tulas,* each holding about 22 kilos (48 pounds). Carrying an average load of 400 kilos, pilots on the Colombia-Mexico run typically earn $100,000 for each flight. Another $150,000 per flight goes to the ground crew responsible for security, unloading and refueling—handsome pay for 15 minutes' work. . . .

2

How to Get Organized

All reporters agree that conscientious organization makes stories easier to write. The variables are time and temperament. Some very disorganized reporters write some very good stories from sketchy notes, and some very organized reporters write some very poor stories from detailed outlines.

It is simpler for a writer who writes one story a month to be organized than a writer who writes three stories a day. But from people who are superorganized, you can learn what you *should* do, and then decide what you *want* to do to change how you work.

For reporters, organization techniques range from a carefully numbered, lettered, color-coded set of manila files to a piled-up heap in the corner. Systematic organization saves time, however, when time may be crucial to get a good story.

Organizing Your Files

You should develop at least three sets of desk-side files — subject files, story files and source files. Legal-size file folders are more adaptable than letter size. You can also color-code your files—red for subject files, green for story files, and blue for source files, for example.

Subject files can be divided into general and specific categories. You might label one file Education, for example, and another file Local High Schools.

The Education file would hold general articles about trends in education or federal legislation that affects education, whereas the Local High Schools file would hold specific information about your community's high schools.

Story files should hold copies of all the documented information you have gathered on each story, along with your notes and a copy (or, for broadcast, a script) of the story when it appeared. For a complicated story with many types of information, use a folder with pockets or a plastic pocket with a zipper to hold loose, undersize material (such as business cards), and photocopy small notes or clippings on 8½-by-11-inch paper. If possible, number and file the research items consecutively and keep a corresponding list of the research documents at the front of the folder so that you don't have to shuffle through each item to find what you want.

Source files should be divided into two kinds—public and personal sources. A public file could be a combination of a business card file and a rotary or other type of card file for your desk. You can keep a second public source file at home or incorporate all the telephone numbers into your personal source file. A personal source file contains names and telephone numbers of the sources you use all the time, as well as the sources you have developed. This proverbial little black book should be portable (pocket- or briefcase-size) and should stay with you always. You can computerize most of this information and store it for easy on-screen access and updating, except for names, addresses, and unlisted phone numbers of private sources.

Organizing a Series of Stories

A reporter with daily deadlines watches each story emerge, shift, stop and start again. Before a prearranged deadline every day, the reporter must write the story. The story often dictates the schedule, as the reporter decides, "This is all I know now. It's time to write."

Use Story Outlines

For a reporter assigned to a three- or four-part series of stories, scheduling is less hurried but often more confusing. Joel Brinkley says, "By the time I decide a story may be worth a series, I've done an interview or two. I spend a week exploring the possibilities, determining what I'm likely to get, how much time and space it's worth.

"Then I write a proposal—basically short story outlines. For example, if I'm writing six stories, my outline tells what each story would say, with some caveats saying, 'I don't know this to be true for sure, but I suspect it's true. I intend to check these records and compile this statistic.'"

Dean Bacquet also uses an outline. "I try to come up with an unusually ambitious outline, and it usually gets pared down. The outline is mainly for myself, but I do present it to an editor. One problem every reporter has is that it's next to impossible to predict how long it's going to take to do a major project. When you start with a huge, nebulous subject, it's really helpful to be thinking in terms of specific stories, to be looking for anecdotes when you interview somebody, to be looking for statistics to make comparisons."

Set a Writing Deadline

With a two- or three-month deadline, when do you stop researching and start writing? Joel Brinkley suggests that you design a story calendar. At the outset, look at the scheduled time and pick the best date to begin writing. Put "Write Today" on that date in a calendar notebook. Then in a separate notebook, make a list of tasks you want to accomplish each day so that you'll be ready to write on schedule ("Interview with Sam Donaldson," "Check Biography Index for George Curry"). Leave at least half of each daily page blank to add to your list of jobs as the story develops.

On May 10, for instance, you might list two interview appointments, three documents you need, and five phone calls you should make. Check off each task as it is accomplished and carry over any tasks you don't finish to May 11 so that you remember.

Joel Brinkley has refined this approach further. He uses a binder with tabbed index dividers for each story in the series. Brinkley makes two lists— "What to Do" and "What to Include"—for each story so that he doesn't overlook a potential source, a possible question or a useful document. He adds to the list as he learns new information, and he checks off the items on the lists as he finishes. "This is a way to realize as you go along how little or how much you have," says Brinkley. "When I'm done, I reread

May 10

1. *Interview with Sam Donaldson   2pm* ✓
2. *Check Who's Who for David Brinkley* ✓
3. *Call Linda Gomez   unavailable - call 5/12*
4. *Call Sandra Thompson* ✓
5. *Call Dean Bacquet* ✓
6. *Check Biography Index for George Curry* ✓
7. *Interview John Martin   4 pm* ✓
8. *Call V U/TEXT for photo* ✓
9. *Check Newsweek article on Westmoreland case* ✓
10. *Call Marylen Schwartz   unavailable - call 5/15*

In this sample list of tasks, eight jobs are finished, and items 3 and 10 will be carried over to another day's list.

every entry to be sure that everything I know has at least been considered for the story."

How to Use an Electronic File

A system like Brinkley's could easily be adapted to an electronic file. Computers have introduced into the newsroom many new methods of record keeping, notetaking, and research (for more information on research methods, see Chapter 4).

Many reporters transcribe their interviews, store their research and keep notes to themselves in the computer system. Some reporters type notes from telephone conversations directly into the computer while they're on the phone, then note any long-distance phone numbers they dial. Confidential information is separately coded so that it cannot be accidentally retrieved by other reporters. Once a reporter has finished an assignment, and made a printout of it, the reporter purges the records from the computer.

A computer also helps a reporter manage secretarial and clerical duties. "Journalists do not typically have secretaries," says Peter Rinearson. "For instance, I would like to write a letter to about 30 people I interviewed [in Japan] to thank them. I wouldn't do this in the U.S., but things operate a little differently culturally in Japan. If I had a secretary, I could do it. Or if I have a computer, I can do it."

An electronic filing system is especially helpful to a team of reporters working on a series. A file can keep one reporter from duplicating work that has been done by another member of the team. An electronic file also helps keep out-of-town reporters updated about new information in a story.

For a series about academic problems among some members of the University of Florida football team, Bill Nottingham says *St. Petersburg Times* reporters developed an electronic master memo file: "Every reporter wrote a memo each day, reporting what had been learned. Then each daily memo file was cross-indexed, for example, under Football Coach Charlie Pell, or Defensive Linemen or Source X."

Nottingham also describes how an electronic filing system kept track of four reporters and an editor working on a series about mass murderer Eugene Stano: "To profile his life, I went to Schenectady, New York, and interviewed police and other officials up there, took pictures of the house he grew up in, then went to the Pennsylvania area, where he went to high school.

"I interviewed friends and the principal of his high school, and got pictures of him playing the bass clarinet in the band. We traveled to Atlanta, too, and took endless trips to Daytona Beach" (where he already had been convicted of murder).

"We took along portable computers so we were constantly, at the end of the day, memo-ing back to our project editor what we had found. If someone found a piece of information, and I was up in New York, the project editor would relay the information up to me by telephone.

"We drafted our end-of-the-day memos in a story style so that whole portions of it could be lifted [to write the story] later. This adds to your speed and helps your accuracy. You're writing something when it is freshest in your mind."

A reporter demonstrates the use of a split screen. Research appears on the right-hand side of the screen, and the reporter uses the left-hand side to write the story.

Another electronic filing method that works well for stories with a lot of dates or statistics is to keep the dates or numbers in one file and write the story in another file. With a split screen, the reporter can call up the chronology of someone's life, for example, on one side of the screen and write the story on the other side of the screen. Then the reporter can double-check the dates in the chronology with the dates in the story.

This split-screen method is particularly useful for reporters who are sharing information on a series. Each reporter inserts information in the central statistical or chronological file as the information becomes available, and then any reporter working on the series can share the information. This helps keep the information consistent in all the stories, even though the series is written by more than one person.

For a series about mass murderer Henry Lee Lucas, reporter Dean Bacquet says, "We came up with the idea of keeping a chronology of his life in our computer system. The chronology started out as bare bones — 'Henry Lee Lucas, born . . .'

"We then called all the newspapers who covered the Lucas case, and every night we'd make entries into the chronology. Then, as we were reporting the story, we would make entries.

"When the time came to write the story, I just called up the chronology on a split screen on the computer." One one side of the screen, Bacquet wrote his story. On the other side of the screen was a dated chronology of Lucas' life. "I didn't have to refer to my notes to see where Lucas was in 1977," Bacquet says. "That's the best organized story situation I've seen."

A Final Word

Organization is one tool a reporter can use to bring order to the dynamic chaos of covering the news. Just think of the admiration you will attract, whenever your editor asks you a question, if you can reach gingerly into your file drawer, pull out a carefully marked folder and say, "Oh, I have the answer right here."

■■■■■ AN INTERVIEWING CASE STUDY

Joel Brinkley
The New York Times

After Joel Brinkley graduated from the University of North Carolina at Chapel Hill, he went to work for Associated Press and then *The Richmond* (Virginia) *News Leader.* In 1978, Brinkley was hired by *The* (Louisville) *Courier-Journal.* He is now Jerusalem Bureau Chief for *The New York Times.*

In 1979, Joel Brinkley was working for *The Courier-Journal,* covering the Jefferson County School Board. His editor decided Brinkley should go to Cambodia and Thailand to find out what Cambodian life was like after the U.S. government left Southeast Asia. Brinkley had 10 days to prepare for the trip, his first overseas assignment.

He read a Bantam paperback, got his shots, and left with a photographer who had traveled in Asia but not in Thailand or Cambodia.

In this example, Brinkley demonstrates his ability to systematically organize a large amount of material into a series of award-winning stories.

"I grew up in northwest Washington, D.C., and went to private school," says Brinkley. "I don't think I have ever been hungry for more than a couple of hours. God knows I had never seen anyone starving to death, let alone seen someone starving, squatting in the mud. My task was to make the reader seem as if he were standing there.

"There were corpses everywhere, tens of thousands of people. The people would come up and paw at us and moan. It was hell. After the first day all I could feel was immense depression, and I had difficulty dealing with it. How was I going to make a reader feel some of this?

"What is there about the situation, the actual physical scene that makes it feel so oppressive? What are the elements of the scene that are going to make the reader feel as I do? What am I hearing? Wails, screams, coughs from TB, buzzing flies on all the little bits of food lying around, the smells of raw sewage, defecation and dead bodies. Rather than say, 'It looks horrible,' I had to ask 'What makes it look horrible?' The photographer shot 76 rolls of film.

"Every night I would go back to my little room. I did not use a tape recorder. I don't like them much because you become too dependent on them. I filled three reporter's notebooks. I put quotes on the left-hand side and description on the right-hand side of the page. I went through my notebooks and circled with red pen what I felt must be in the story. Then I made a list of what should be in the story by page number and notebook number. I don't do outlines. The first three stories took me five days to write.

"I got typhoid in one of the camps. You have to pick three diseases for vaccinations. I didn't pick typhoid. I had lost 15 pounds and was just out of bed. I would write a draft, make a printout and take it home, and then go back to it after dinner. I kept thinking, 'The paper spent $4,000 to send us to Cambodia. We had better come back with something good.'"

The first story in a four-part series ran in *The Courier-Journal* on December 2, 1979. In 1980, 27-year-old Brinkley and photographer Jay Mather won the Pulitzer Prize for international reporting for their series, "Living the Cambodian Nightmare."

Living the Cambodian Nightmare
By Joel Brinkley
Courier-Journal Staff Writer

Gaunt, glassy-eyed and possessionless, they crouch in the heat amid thousands of others, hungry and diseased. They stoop over small, dry plots of rock-hard soil. And they wait.

They wait in tight lines for hours to get today's ration of food from international relief agencies: a bowl of rice gruel, two bananas, a bucket of brown drinking water.

They wait for doctors to heal them.

Some wait for news of family, though many know their relatives are dead; they remember watching brothers and sisters, parents and children being murdered, or struggling for a final breath before starvation. . . .

"It is very sad about my country," said Say Khol, a 30-year-old man who once taught English in Phnom Penh. He was sitting in Cambodia's Samet Meanchey refugee camp a half-mile from the Thai border, drawing in the dirt as he talked.

"Small boy, he no have anything to learn. Old man, he no have anything to eat. Cambodia is only here. This all that is left of my country. Soon this will be gone, too."

Like many Cambodians, Say spoke English often "until Pol Pot. Since then, I scared to speak one word or I be killed. I forget so much."

Pol Pot is the communist commander whose Khmer Rouge soldiers overthrew the American-backed military government of Gen. Lon Nol in 1975. (Khmer is the Cambodian race, as Anglo-Saxon is the British race.) After the overthrow, Pol Pot's soldiers began executing everyone with any hint of wealth or education—especially those who spoke a foreign language.

The executions were supposed to purge centuries of Western influence and remake Cambodia into a self-sufficient, rural society.

Death came swiftly from machetes and bullets, or slowly from prolonged torture. More than a million Cambodians died that first year.

Some were hung upside down by their feet, their heads submerged in buckets of water. They remained alive as long as their neck muscles could hold their faces out of the water. Still others were publicly disemboweled.

Children were chained together, then buried alive.

Say, a handsome young man, had been a lieutenant in Lon Nol's army. But when the Khmer Rouge forces approached Phnom Penh, "I threw away my uniform, put on clothes to look like an ordinary farmer and tried to leave the city."

The executions had already begun.

"I saw many, many people killed, hit on the back of the neck with a bamboo knife. They threw the bodies into huge, big piles in the middle of the street.

"I saw my friends in those piles. . . ."

3

How to Find the Research Information You Need

In the 1957 movie "Desk Set," Katharine Hepburn plays a reference librarian at a media company. Spencer Tracy plays an efficiency expert hired by the company to streamline the reference system. His answer is a complete wall-size computer that can instantly answer any reference question Hepburn asks. Hepburn types in a question, and the computer prints out the answer in less than a minute.

More than a quarter of a century later, every reporter must envy the "Desk Set" computer with instant answers to any reference question. Despite today's technology, this omniscient computer still exists only in fantasy. Today, a reporter still must look for answers to difficult research questions in books, magazines, reports and government documents. And most of those resources are still in the library—whether the library is a staff of reference librarians working at your newspaper, a local public library, or a library you call up on your computer screen.

Reporters who can find information through their computers using *database searching* and *information retrieval* must still be able to define what they want to know, just like the reporter working through a public library or with an in-house librarian. The core of good reporting today is the same as in 1957—the ability to find accurate information quickly.

Five Research Puzzles

Where would you look, for instance, if you faced the following assignments?

1. Your editor tells you on Monday morning that you will be leaving on Friday for the Middle East to do a four-part series on terrorist activities. You have never been to the Middle East—in fact, you have never traveled outside your state. Where would you look for a listing of books and articles about terrorism in the Middle East?

2. The city zoo in your town announces that the panda bear is pregnant. The baby was conceived by artificial insemination. For your story, you want to add facts about the first panda ever conceived by artificial insemination. You think it happened in China, but you can't remember the panda's name. Where do you look?

3. Fifteen separate farming operations in your area report that several of their three-month-old piglets suddenly stopped eating and then died two days later. Local veterinarians can't determine why the pigs died, and you need an expert to help you understand the possible explanations. Whom would you call?

4. The local high school announces an Indian festival honoring Crazy Horse. You can't remember who Crazy Horse was, why he is an Indian folk hero, or when he died. Where do you look?

5. Apartment owners in your town decide to take the first step to raise rents by introducing an ordinance before the city council to eliminate rent controls. You look in the telephone book, but there is no organization in your area that represents tenants' rights. How can you find a spokesperson for the tenants' point of view?

If you were an inexperienced reporter with these five assignments, you might react to each situation like this:

1. *Middle East assignment.* You go to the local bookstore and buy all the paperbacks you can find on the Middle East that show a listing for terrorism in the table of contents.

2. *Baby panda.* You decide that the name of the first panda conceived by artificial insemination isn't important, so you write your story without the name.

3. *Pig deaths.* You report the speculation of two local veterinarians on the cause of the disease, although they admit to you they have never treated a swine disease that kills young pigs so quickly.

4. *Crazy Horse.* You call the student organizer for the festival and ask her who Crazy Horse was and when he died.

5. *Rent controls*. You report that the apartment owners will appear before the city council but that there is no apparent opposition to the new ordinance.

Although these solutions are quick and easy, your stories will be uninteresting, incomplete, shallow and even inaccurate. The Middle East background will be helpful but too general. The panda's name isn't crucial, but it would make the story more interesting. The veterinarians cannot give you any useful information other than what is already generally known.

The high school student says that Crazy Horse died in the late 1700s, which is what you report (but she's wrong), and she can't give you any details about his life. And when your article appears about the city council meeting, three tenants' association members from a nearby county, as well as the statewide association president, telephone your editor to ask why they weren't called about the story. They are on record as opposed to any changes in city rent control ordinances and plan to appear at the meeting.

A reporter who uses the easiest research approach often cheats the reader. In the first three examples, the stories are less interesting because of the missing details. In the fourth story, the student gave you wrong information about Crazy Horse, and in the fifth example, you have denied your readers an essential point of view on the rent control debate.

Careful, systematic research makes the difference between a story that merely records and a story that teaches, explains and enlightens. To become a better reporter, you should learn how to mimic the people who answer other people's questions every day—librarians. Librarians don't know the answer to every question. They simply know how and where to find accurate answers quickly.

Sources are crucial to every reporter. The first source to cultivate for all of your research dilemmas is a good reference librarian. Librarians serve as switching stations, directing each question to its answer. For you, this switching station may be available at your computer, at an in-house library, or at the other end of your telephone. You also can pursue your research at a university library or a large public library if you have one nearby.

Analyze the Research You Need

No matter where the answer is, you must first analyze (1) what information you want to know, (2) why you want to know the information, (3) how you will use the information, (4) how much time you have for research.

1. *What information do you want to know?* Do you need a fact? Do you want a date? Do you need a phone number? Do you need the name of an expert? Do you want background? Which statistics do you need? Make a list of the research you need.

2. *Why do you want to know the information?* Is the information critical to your story? Secondary? Interesting but optional? Rank your list of research items from most to least important.

3. *How will you use the information?* Will you quote the information, the source, both? Must you include the statistic or the date to make your story complete? Will you use the information to frame interview questions? Mark each item with its possible role in your story.

4. *How much time do you have for research?* Do you have four minutes, four hours or four weeks? On a breaking story with a quick deadline, you can follow news service reports and use the telephone. When you have more time, decide which method of research will be most productive before you begin. Will you rely on the telephone? How much time will you have to review what has already been written about the subject? Must you check or copy government documents? Will you be able to review court decisions? Set a realistic deadline.

Quick Help

Ideally, you will have all the research time you need to find out about a topic. But realistically, you often face an assignment with an hour or less to become an expert. Here are some quick references that reporters find useful.

Ask the Experts

If you're assigned an interview with an expert on a subject that's new to you and you have to be there in an hour, how can you prepare? Call another specialist in the same field as your interviewee—an attorney who practices the same kind of law or a doctor who practices the same kind of medicine, for example. Call the nearest university public information office and ask for an expert on the subject you want to know about. Then ask the expert: "What are the current issues being debated by specialists in your field?" or "If you were interviewing someone about this topic, what questions would you ask?" Add the expert's questions to your own questions for a better interview.

Telephone Books

Your local telephone book leads you to local sources, but what if you live in Arizona and you want to find a modeling agency in New York? If you dial the New York information operator, you're allowed three minutes (the operator's time limit to find an answer), and the operator does not have classified listings for businesses. Instead, visit the largest public library in your area, where you will find telephone directories for most major U.S. cities and some foreign cities.

A different kind of telephone book is *Polk's Directory*. This annual publication, compiled for most major cities, is a favorite of police detectives and real estate agents. If you have a telephone number or an address, you can find the owner through *Polk's*.

Polk's lists telephone numbers sequentially. The first listing might be 333–1000, for example, and the next listing would be 333–1001. Shown after each phone number is the name of the person to whom the phone belongs, with an address and usually an occupation. Streets are listed alphabetically and sequentially so that 1001 Almond Street comes before 1002 Almond Street, for example, and Bridge Street follows Almond. Listed after the address are the name, occupation and often the telephone number of people living at that address. Local telephone companies also publish reverse directories; often these are more up to date than *Polk's*. Check both.

Library Telephone Reference Services

If you have a question that can be answered in three minutes, the New York Public Library Reference Service will help. Dial (212)340-0849. Reference librarians handle 1,000 requests a day. Working from more than 1,000 reference sources, the librarians will answer trivia questions ("What metals aren't magnetic?"), requests for dates ("When was Marilyn Monroe born?"), or grammar and spelling questions ("What's the difference between affect and effect?"). Other major cities, such as San Francisco, Detroit, Chicago and Washington, D.C., offer similar services.

Next, remember that the great compilers of statistics are national, state and local governments. The *Federal Directory,* updated every six months, lists federal employees by name, address and agency. Most of the information is for Washington, D.C., but the directory also lists some regional offices. Check with the agency's public information officer for current statistics. Use your local *state, county* and *city government directories* to find government public information people.

Almanacs

For a quick statistical desk reference, nothing beats an almanac, such as *Information Please Almanac* or *The World Almanac and Book of Facts*. You can learn who is the current governor of New Hampshire, which are the world's most notable active volcanoes, or who caught the largest saltwater fish last year. The editors of each almanac decide what to include, so check the general index to decide which one will help you the most.

Gazetteers

If you wanted to locate Dismal Swamp, Foul Bay or Throgs Neck, where would you look? The *Columbia Lippincott Gazetteer of the World* or *Webster's New Geographical Dictionary* could tell you. Gazetteers show pronunciation and geographical location with a brief description for each listing, including cities and towns as well as waterways and important landmarks. (Dismal Swamp, 30 miles long, runs through North Carolina. Foul Bay is an inlet of the Red Sea on the east coast of Egypt. Throgs Neck is a peninsula in the Bronx borough of New York City.)

Desk Encyclopedias

The *New Columbia Encyclopedia* and *Macmillan's Concise Dictionary of World History* can quickly answer historical questions. Both books can help you with assignment 4 (p. 22). Crazy Horse died in 1877. He was an American Sioux Indian chief of the Oglala tribe who led the defeat of Custer at the Battle of the Little Bighorn.

Press Directories

Ayer's Directory of Newspapers, Magazines and Trade Publications; Bacon's Publicity Checker; Editor and Publisher Yearbook and *Broadcasting Yearbook,* to name a few, can help you find a quick contact with reliable information in a distant town. You can find the *Tundra Times* (Anchorage, Alaska) or the *Park County Republican and Fairplay Flume* (Fairplay, Colorado) or the *Nebraska Smoke-Eater* (a magazine for firefighters published in Pierce, Nebraska).

Maps

Many newsrooms post local and regional street maps on the wall. Buy some for your car. The first purchase you should make when you arrive in an unfamiliar town is a street map.

The First Step—Where Project Research Begins

Quick reference sources help you meet imminent deadlines, but for a project story a reporter usually begins by "calling up the clips." You might phone the company librarian and say, "Send me everything you have on . . .," or you might shuffle through the clippings yourself. After reading background about your subject, you may be tempted to use other people's clever lines rather than writing your own story. Instead, review the clippings to help you:

1. Remember what has happened.
2. Collect a list of people to interview.
3. See which aspects of the story have been reported before but, more important, which aspects have been overlooked.
4. Check whether the incident is limited to your community or is part of a national or international trend or movement.

Information Retrieval

In "Desk Set," Katharine Hepburn and Spencer Tracy innocently anticipated in 1957 the widespread use of computer indexes today to help reporters find what they need. With database searching, a librarian or a reporter can look at each listing from an index (such as the *Education Index,* the *Social Sciences Index,* or the *Reader's Guide to Periodical Literature)* on a computer screen instead of in a book. The listings are categorized by subject, title, author, even date—an on-the-screen marvel that puts the library at a reporter's fingertips.

The greatest advantage of electronic information retrieval is quick access to an enormous amount of detail—the name of the president of Du Pont and the members of the board of directors, the current population of Greece, or the winner of the 1988 Olympic women's 100-meter run. Hepburn and Tracy would be proud.

At a large metropolitan newspaper with information retrieval, a reporter types a coded request for the available information on a specific subject into the computer or asks the library to do the search. Many large broadcast stations also have introduced information retrieval into their newsrooms. The screen shows a list of available items with a brief description of each item, and the reporter or librarian can then tell the computer to print copies of the items they want.

Computer screens can be used to research stories through information retrieval.

At the *Los Angeles Times,* a reporter can use the *Times'* clipping files as well as the major database indexes, such as NEXIS and LEXIS. NEXIS indexes Associated Press, United Press International, the *Encyclopaedia Britannica, The Washington Post,* and *The New York Times* as well as the *Japan Economic Journal* and the *Current Digest of the Soviet Press.*

NEXIS can find articles from magazines, such as *Chemical Engineering, Nuclear News,* and *Oil & Gas Journal* as well as *Business Week* and *U.S. News & World Report.* Even specialized newsletters, such as *Coal Week International* and *Electrical Marketing,* are included in the NEXIS system.

Mead Data Central, which owns NEXIS, claims that one research request for information about oysters turned up 57 stories in 15 seconds. One story reported that the world's largest oyster farm, the Kahuku Seafood Plantation in Hawaii, produced 250,000 oysters in one month. A second story featured the world's fastest oyster shucker, Ruth Smith, who removed the shells of 24 oysters in three minutes and 51 seconds.

LEXIS, intended for attorneys but also used by many major newspapers, offers current superior, circuit and federal court decisions, as well as reports of federal bankruptcy court decisions. LEXIS searches can even include British and French court files.

VU/TEXT indexes many large regional newspapers, such as *The Philadelphia Inquirer, The Miami Herald* and the *Detroit Free Press,* but its database also includes *The Washington Post*. VU/TEXT lists articles in reverse chronological order, with the most recent articles first, so that a reporter can get the newest information and then search for background.

A reporter working without in-house information retrieval can use a university library or a large public library for a computer search. If you take your project to the library, however, you also must take your wallet.

Many news organizations underwrite reporters' computer research, and information retrieval can be costly. An hour of research time costs $20 or more. The time is calculated by the number of minutes the retrieval service takes to transmit the information to the terminal. Still, this investment in computer time can save you hours, even days, of research working by yourself.

Research Limitations

Information retrieval saves time, minimizes error, and offers material that is usually much more up to date than traditional indexes. Besides cost, however, there are some other limitations of information retrieval that every reporter should understand.

1. *Information retrieval often offers too much information.* One recent search for articles about diet and weight reduction turned up 328 listings for one month. You must be careful to limit the information you want. You're likely to get 3,000 citations for one month if you ask for all the information about the president of the United States. If you confine the search to the president's public statements about Israel in 1991, you will get a shorter, more useful list.

2. *Many citations are duplicates.* If, for instance, Associated Press carries a story and the story appears in *The Washington Post* and *The New York Times*, a computer search often lists all three stories under different headlines even though they are identical. To counteract this problem when you research a topic that turns up an overwhelming number of listings, you can request a sample list (perhaps 50) of the most promising articles by title to narrow your choices before you request the complete articles.

3. *Information retrieval is relatively new.* Most database search companies began business after 1975, so the information in their indexes includes items that appeared only after each service began. An information retrieval company that began in 1985, for example, would list articles from 1985 publications, but not from 1980.

4. *Mistakes are multiplied.* Stories with inaccurate statistics, partial information or the wrong information are filed alongside accurate stories. This increases the chance that one error will be picked up repeatedly. Remember to independently verify any questionable facts.

"Nine times out of 10 nobody ever checks," says Bill Endicott. "For instance, another reporter and I did a story during the 1960s about the students who burned the Bank of America in Santa Barbara. Our story said that the student government at the University of Santa Barbara had withdrawn its money from this branch of the Bank of America the night before it was burned.

"It turned out that the student government had never had their money in that bank. We based our story on information we were given by university officials, as I recall. That clipping is now in our file in Los Angeles, and someday somebody is going to do a retrospective on the Santa Barbara riots and pull out the clips and repeat that error all over again."

No matter where you begin research—in your own files, in the clip file or at your computer—remember that conscientious, original research often distinguishes an adequate reporter from an excellent reporter. Carefully researched details say to a reader, "I care enough as a reporter about you and about my story to get the best, most accurate information I can."

The Second Step—From General to Specific

To research an unfamiliar subject, your librarian works from the general to the specific. You should do the same. (You also will find some research help here for the story assignments on p. 22). Depending on your knowledge of a subject, follow this research order:

1. *A reference book guide.* If you face a completely new subject, don't rush to the bookstore. Instead, do what a librarian does—check *A Guide to Reference Books*. In one average-size volume, this guide lists and reviews the most widely used research books, indexed by subject area. Under Political Science (General Works, Bibliography), for example, you can find the best source of information for your unexpected trip to the Middle East (see assignment 1, p. 22). *A Guide to Reference Books* tells you that a book called *The Literature of Terrorism* lists "3,869 books, articles, government documents and documents of international organizations, grouped by

subject—tactics, philosophies, guerrilla warfare, the media, and terrorism in geographic regions and countries." For any unfamiliar issue assignment, start with this guide.

2. *A general encyclopedia.* An encyclopedia, such as the *Encyclopaedia Britannica* or *Encyclopedia Americana,* will familiarize you with the subject from a layperson's viewpoint.

3. *A specialized encyclopedia.* An encyclopedia for a specific subject can give you more specialized information than a general encyclopedia. The *Encyclopedia of Computer Science and Engineering,* for example, explains how different types of computers work.

4. *General magazine and newspaper indexes.* To see the national scope of your issue, check general magazine indexes, such as the *Magazine Index* (available on microfilm and through information retrieval), *Reader's Guide to Periodical Literature,* and indexes for newspapers with national circulation, such as the *Los Angeles Times, The Wall Street Journal,* and *The New York Times.*

5. *A specialized index.* A guide to journals and periodicals devoted to a specific subject, such as *Business Periodicals Index* or *Agriculture Index,* helps you understand current debate about your subject from magazine articles. The *Monthly Catalog of United States Government Publications* gives a subject listing of pamphlets and reports recently published by the nation's largest publisher.

6. *A specialized dictionary.* To decipher unfamiliar jargon, use a specialized dictionary, such as *A Dictionary of the Language of Sports* or the *Dictionary of Economic and Statistical Terms.*

7. *A specialized handbook.* The only reference manual directed specifically at a journalist's challenges is *The Reporter's Handbook,* which will teach you how to research more than 500 types of public documents, including how to trace who owns a specific piece of property; how to investigate state and federal law enforcement records; and how to document medical malpractice. *The Reporter's Handbook* is compiled by Investigative Reporters and Editors, Inc.

The Third Step—Focusing the Research

With your collection of clippings (from either the library or your computer) and a fat background file from your general research, you are ready for the third research step. Ask yourself:

1. Do I need facts?
2. Do I need personal profile background?
3. Do I need issue information?

Factual Research

The goal of most factual research is a number, a date or a place. This is the most specific type of research, but once you learn where the knowledge genie hides these goodies, factual research is easy.

Statistical Abstract of the United States is the grandmother of all American numbers books. Some of the tables in the *Statistical Abstract,* which is published by the U.S. Bureau of the Census, go back to 1787. You can find birth, death, divorce and marriage rates, and any other information covered by the U.S. Census, as well as some comparisons to international statistics. You can learn, for example, the average salaries for police officers and firefighters; how many people died in motorcycle accidents in a specific year; which animals are on the endangered species list; or how world military expenditures compare over a 10-year period. *Pocket Data Book U.S.A.* is an abridged, quick-reference version of *Statistical Abstract.*

U.N. Statistical Yearbook and *Demographic Yearbook* are the international companions of *Statistical Abstract.* Go to the *Statistical Yearbook* for industrial information, such as the average wages paid for a specific profession or how much money an average family earns in a year. *Demographic Yearbook* emphasizes cultural information, such as marriage, birth and death rates, and each country's ethnic composition.

Public Affairs Information Service Bulletin (PAIS) is an excellent up-to-date complement to *Statistical Abstract, U.N. Statistical Yearbook,* and *Demographic Yearbook,* which sometimes run two to three years behind. PAIS indexes current political, economic and international affairs articles in 1,400 magazines, pamphlets and documents.

Facts on File is a looseleaf weekly news bulletin covering international and national news, sports, even obituaries. If you remember the month and year an event occurred, *Facts on File* is invaluable and quick.

Personality Research

More than any other type of story, a profile directly reflects the breadth of a reporter's research. Poorly researched profiles repeat well-known facts and tired anecdotes. Well-researched profiles glitter with new information, quotes and description.

"I once interviewed Samuel J. Lefrak, who built Lefrak City in Queens, New York," says Stuart Dim. "I found out from a newspaper society column that he had visited Japan several times. This eventually led to my discovering, during the interview, that he had transported, rock by rock, a Japanese garden to his home on Long Island. The fact that I mentioned his visits to Japan prompted him to tell me about the rock garden, which helped me to write a more descriptive picture of how he lived."

To learn all you can about someone, check these sources:

The most comprehensive biographical guide is *Biographical Dictionaries Master Index*. This index lists more than 750,000 people who are cataloged in some biographical directory. For instance, if you look up columnist and author Erma Bombeck, you learn that you can find her biography in the *Current Biography Yearbook*. Other indexes to biographical listings are *Biography Index, Current Biography,* and *National Cyclopedia of American Biography*.

Who's Who and its variations (such as *Who's Who in American Education, Who's Who in Engineering, Who's Who in Rock Music, Who's Who in Boxing*) are the most accessible biographical directories to well-known personalities and public figures. Written by the biographees, the *Who's Who* listings are a good guide to how well-known people think about themselves. (People who were well known, but no longer are, appear in *Who Was Who*.)

A new *Who's Who* is *The Animals' Who's Who*, which features "over 1,100 animals of renown from life and letters—animals in myth and legend, literature and children's stories." If you wanted a specific answer to assignment 2 (p. 22), this reference would tell you that the first giant panda bred by artificial insemination was Yuanjing, born at the Beijing (Peking) Zoo in the fall of 1978. She weighed a quarter of a pound. (You could also learn that the name of Charlie Chaplin's co-star in the 1918 movie "A Dog's Life" was Scraps, billed as a "thoroughbred mongrel," and that the name of the gorilla in the 1932 movie "Murders in the Rue Morgue" was Erik.)

The *International Year Book and Statesmen's Who's Who* covers important world figures. U.S. senators and members of Congress write their own listings for the *Congressional Directory*. Many state governments publish a biographical booklet, such as the *California Blue Book*, about state and local officials and legislators.

Some other very useful specialized biographical guides are *Contemporary Authors, American Men and Women of Science, Directory of American Scholars, World Biography, Celebrity Register,* and *The Address Book: How to Reach Anyone Who is Anyone*. Also remember that many people have more than one occupation. Elected officials are often attorneys. Authors also can be athletes. Doctors also can be artists. Be alert for any biographical information that signals overlapping occupations.

Other sources of possible documentary information, depending on the public information access laws where you live, include:

1. *Court records*—for information on divorces, insurance claims, bankruptcies, wills, criminal charges and pending lawsuits.

2. *Legislative indexes and hearing transcripts*—to find people who have testified on the record as advocates or opponents of an issue, and to analyze arguments for proposed changes in the law.

3. *Business license applications*—for the name and address of the owner of a local business, and to find out whether the business is affiliated with or franchised by a national corporation.

4. *Professional license applications*—to learn about lawyers, doctors, dentists, teachers, accountants, private investigators, cosmetologists and real estate agents, who must obtain a license to practice their trade. License applications often show name, address, age and place of birth.

5. *Partnership or incorporation applications*—to learn the names and addresses of the owners and/or officers of a business, as well as how long the business has been operating.

6. *Speeches*—to quote and analyze public pronouncements and on-the-record statements.

7. *Budget documents*—to "follow the paper trail," which is an investigative reporter's credo. By showing the amount of money a public agency gives to a program, a budget reflects the importance of that program to the elected or appointed officials who wrote the budget. Budgets also often list officials' salaries and office expenses.

8. *Driver's license and motor vehicle records*—unavailable to reporters in many states, unless you have a friend in law enforcement. If your state gives you access, you can learn someone's social security number, address, age, and the make and model of the person's car.

9. *Arrest records*—list the suspect's name, address, date and place of birth, sex, race and occupation. Arrest records also show the name of the complainant or victim and the name of the arresting officer.

10. *Financial disclosure statements*—show personal finances for public officials, and any indications of conflict of interest—that a legislator on the banking committee serves as a board member of a local bank, for instance.

11. *Voter registration records*—list party affiliation, address and polling place.

12. *Birth and death records*—often available only by a request directly from the person or his or her family, these records list names and addresses of parents on the date of the child's birth, parents' occupation, and the attending physician.

13. *Tax records*—property tax records reflect whether someone's taxes are current and may reflect the current value of someone's home. Personal federal and state tax records usually are confidential.

14. *Probate records*—court documents may list names of heirs, as well as the value of real estate, personal property, stocks, bonds and business holdings of the person who died.[1]

Once you have checked every possible documented source of information about your biographee (and you may find no printed sources at all), ask your subject to send you any standard printed background material. Before you formally interview your subject, consider contacting the following: friends, enemies, church members, family members, military buddies, professional colleagues, college roommates and club associates. Your last formal interview will be with the subject of your profile.

Also find out what your subject does for recreation so that you can interview a tennis partner, for instance, or the members of a Saturday volleyball team. One reporter interviewed his subject's tax accountant. Another reporter interviewed the local librarian to find out which books his subject checked out.

Issue Research

"Can we get a local angle on this story?" Editors often ask their reporters to try to explain a broad national issue (such as cuts in the federal welfare program) or a spreading national trend (such as an increasing birth rate). The editor wants the reporter to find local people who are affected by the change or a local expert who can explain the trend. With such a large focus, how can you find the appropriate people quickly? Here are some helpers:

1. *A social services organization directory.* How can you present both sides of an issue, such as tenants' rights, if you can't find a local organization to defend rent controls? The answer is *Social Service Organizations and Agencies,* which lists national organizations and federal and state agencies by subject. This directory includes listings for child welfare, civil rights, drug abuse, marriage, divorce, sexuality and veterans' affairs. Under tenants' rights (assignment 5, p. 22), you could find the National Tenants Union, with 50 state tenants' rights group members. (You could also find the National Center for Computer Crime Data, the Employee Relocation Council, and Mistresses Anonymous, "a self-help organization for women involved with married men.")

2. *A college directory.* A scholar can give you an understandable explanation of a complicated, technical issue or an analytical, critical opinion about an intricate controversy. Four college directories will help you find a scholar. The *Education Directory, Colleges and Universities* lists all two- and four-year colleges and universities. You can call the college public relations officer to help you find an expert. The *Directory of American Scholars* gives biographies of humanities scholars (English, history, speech, drama, foreign languages, linguistics, philosophy, religion, law). *American Men and Women of Science* covers notable scientific scholars (food and nutrition, botany, biology, chemistry, ecology, archaeology, geology). Social science scholars (history, government, sociology, psychology, criminology) appear in *American Men and Women of Science: Social and Behavioral Sciences.*

3. *An association directory.* The *Encyclopedia of Associations* lists nearly 15,000 trade associations, professional societies, labor unions, and fraternal and patriotic organizations. When you need a business expert, a hobbyist or a professional specialist, this directory helps you take an issue from the general to the specific, from national to local.

   If you need an expert on swine diseases (assignment 3, p. 22), this directory tells you about the American Association of Swine Practitioners and Veterinarians. Located in Des Moines, Iowa, this association's 1,780 members devote themselves to swine health and nutrition. (This directory also can give you information, for example, that will ignite reader interest in the Spark Plug Collectors of America, uncover inside information from the Allied Underwear Association, and help you learn about fish from the International Fancy Guppy Association.)

A Final Word

Well-documented research gives you the background you need to ask good questions, to match your interviewee's answers with what your research tells you. To be a truly good researcher, you can't be satisfied with just *an* answer. You must always look until you find *the best* answer.

■■■■■ A RESEARCH CASE STUDY

Kristin Gilger
The Times-Picayune

Kristin Gilger graduated with honors from the University of Nebraska with a master's degree in journalism. She worked for *The* (Charleston, South Carolina) *News and Courier* and the *St. Cloud* (Minnesota) *Times* before she was hired by *The* (New Orleans, Louisiana) *Times-Picayune*. Gilger is now assistant to the editor at the *Times-Picayune*.

Kristin Gilger had been in a bureau of *The Times-Picayune* less than a year when she wrote this story. This is a good example of how a reporter can put together research information about someone's personal life very quickly.

"I [once] had to write a profile of a man I had never met or even heard of before getting the assignment. I had to do the story in about four hours. The subject, George Oubre, made himself unavailable for comment.

"So where do you start? First, I checked news clips for background information and, most importantly, names of people associated with Oubre in the past. With the help of another reporter, I called them all—a former law partner, those who worked on his election campaign, a man who accompanied Oubre on a recent trip, friends, even his wife, although she wouldn't comment.

"I then went to his office, even though I knew he wasn't there. I got friendly with the secretary. She gave me more names and a biography. I was unsuccessful at getting a picture.

"Acting on tips, I checked court records on his divorce and remarriage and called a local bank to confirm he was just named a director. I also checked campaign contribution records filed by the governor, for whom Oubre had campaigned.

"My approach when calling these people was, 'I don't know much about the man, and I'd appreciate anything you can tell me. My main concern is what kind of a person he is. ————just told me that you know him. How would you describe him? I understand you accompanied him on a trip, were a former law partner, worked in his campaign.'

"As you can see from the story, it is possible to profile a man without ever talking to him."

Indictment Clouding Oubre's Day in the Sun
By Kris Gilger and Barri Marsh

George Oubre was a man on his way back.

Oubre, 53, who left the state in 1975 under a political and personal cloud, was making a strong comeback in state politics under the banner of Gov.-elect Edwin W. Edwards, friends and associates of Oubre said Friday.

But a federal grand jury brought the clouds back Friday, indicting the former state senator on charges of conspiring and making false statements to several Jefferson Parish banks to get loans. . . .

Last week, Oubre accompanied port staff and commissioners on a trip to Costa Rica to develop foreign trade. He represented Edwards' staff on the trip.

Oubre also was recently named to the board of directors of the Riverlands National Bank in La-Place, a bank spokeswoman confirmed Friday.

His future looked bright—until Friday.

One longtime friend, Warren Landry, a former St. Charles Parish councilman, described him as a "man who loves his fun."

Landry, who also went on the Edwards' European trip, said news of the indictment was a shock. "I just left him at the airport yesterday. We've been together for a week."

Oubre gave no indication that he was troubled during the trip, Landry said, describing him as cheerful and "the leader of the partiers.". . .

As a resident of the River Parishes Oubre has been active in civic affairs. He is past president of the East St. Charles Chamber of Commerce and the Norco Chamber of Commerce and a former member of the Kiwanis Club of the River Parishes.

Oubre is from a prominent St. Charles Parish family. His father, Lezin Oubre, was employed by Shell Oil Co., Norco, and served on the South Louisiana Port Commission for many years. His brother, Lezin Oubre Jr., has long been active in the St. Charles Democratic organization. His uncle is 29th Judicial District Judge C. William Bradley.

4

How to Take Notes

A reporter is a human video and audio recorder of events. To keep an accurate record is the reporter's responsibility. A television or radio reporter who doesn't record the images or sounds of a story doesn't have the story. A print reporter can choose whether to record an interview in a notebook or on a tape recorder or both.

The first test of an interviewee is his or her reaction to your notebook. When you start taking notes, you become a critic who silently gives the interviewee messages ("Well, that quote wasn't particularly interesting because I didn't write it down," or "Can't you talk a little more slowly?" or "I wrote down every word. Those are good quotes.")

A normal conversation runs at a speed of more than 100 words a minute. A nervous interviewee may talk faster, and a relaxed conversation may run a little slower, but even a fast notetaker can write only 25 to 50 words a minute. How will you keep up?

Develop Your Own Shorthand

Shorthand is a great asset to any reporter, but most reporters rely on their own form of speedwriting. Whatever method you use, take notes during the entire interview, even if what you're noting are descriptive details—someone's thin, freckled hands or distinctive, aquiline nose. Sometimes an interviewee who sees you stop writing will stop talking.

"Some reporters stop writing, look bored, or tap their foot when the interviewee gets off the track," says Kristin Gilger. "I keep writing. I take down *everything* that is said in an interview. Sometimes I don't want the person to know exactly what I am interested in anyway." Try to spotlight important quotes as you take notes. You can star (*) them or put a quick check (√) in the margin.

To practice notetaking and to develop your own form of shorthand, record a radio or television news broadcast on tape while you take notes. Try to write down all proper names, nouns, verbs and any particularly interesting adjectives. You can omit articles (the, an) and prepositions (of, for). Then transcribe your notes, add the articles and prepositions, and match your notes to the recording. Were your notes accurate? What did you miss? Continue to practice to improve your speed and accuracy.

Notebooks

When you introduce a notebook into an interview, you signal to your interviewee that you are ready to work. On a breaking story, you must keep your notebook ready, but in a scheduled interview, keep your notebook in a pocket or briefcase at first. Then bring out the notebook during the early conversation as you say, "That's very interesting," and write down a small fact. The notebook becomes a friend to the interviewee instead of an adversary.

A notebook can even become a physical barrier. A tense reporter sometimes sits forward stiffly on the edge of a chair, holding up a notepad and pen and hurriedly saying, "Uh-huh, uh-huh." The interviewee "has a real sense that the reporter is just trying to get a quote," says Joel Brinkley. "That's the quickest way to ensure that somebody will not be useful and candid."

Most reporters use a hand-size, 4-by-8-inch or 5-by-8-inch reporter's notebook with wider lines on the paper than on regular binder paper. Instead of pens, many reporters like retractable disposable pencils, which offer an important advantage—an eraser. (Always keep some extras with you in case you run out of lead.) Pencils also write under almost any conditions, including uphill. Reporters typically write on the front of the paper, flip the paper and the notebook cover backward, and write on the back of the first sheet before going on to the second sheet. This timesaver also limits noisy paper shuffling.

Some reporters like to use an 8½-by-11-inch notepad for long sit-down interviews. A tablet this size rests comfortably on your knee and allows room for you to write notes from the interview on the left-hand two-thirds of the page and leave a wide right-hand margin to jot down a description of the interviewee (that large nose wart) or of the room where the interview

Sm rptrs use 8 1/2 x 11 ntpad 4 long sit-dn int. Rests cmftbly on ne + rm to rite notes frm. int. on lft-hand 2/3 of pg + lv. wide rt-hnd margin – jot dn. desc. of int. -e (nose wart) or rm whr int tks plc (frmd pr hrt-covd bxr shrts mt interest rdr)

The last paragraph on page 41 might look like this in a reporter's notebook.

takes place (the framed pair of heart-covered boxer shorts might interest your readers).

On-the-spot interviews offer another type of challenge. "When I was in journalism school, I practiced the relaxed, in-the-office, sit-down interview," says one reporter. "Then for my first year as a reporter, I never did an interview sitting down. I was usually at breaking news events—fires or robberies—and I was always standing up." This is why a hand-size notebook is important.

List of Questions

Whenever possible, you should prepare a list of questions for your interview beforehand (see Chapter 6), but keep the list separate from your notebook. Otherwise, you will be flipping from the front of your notebook, where you've written your questions, to the middle or back of the notebook, where you're writing the answers.

Write out your questions in longhand, and then transfer them to another list containing only keywords to remind yourself what the questions are during the interview. Especially with complicated questions, interviewers tend to read their questions word for word, which interrupts the impression that the interview is a conversation. With a keyword list, you can glance at the questions, follow your interview plan, and keep your eyes on the interviewee. When a new idea emerges from the interview, however, be willing to change your approach and pursue the new information.

Do not number your questions or check the questions off as you go. A quick-eyed interviewee is likely to glance at your list, see 14 numbered, two-paragraph questions, and realize that you are on number 4. The interviewee, hoping to reach the end of the list before midnight, will collapse the answers into short, staccato remarks. This does not encourage an interviewee to relax enough to ramble into interesting, unexpected comments.

A short list of keyword, unnumbered questions, however, is an important road map for you to use at the end of the interview for a quick check that you have covered what you planned to ask. You can always skip a prepared question or ask new questions, but by reviewing your list before you leave the interview, you remember to ask what you felt was important before the interview began. "What I do, invariably, is write out my questions," says George Curry. "When I go to an interview, I generally don't look at them. I don't know whether it's a security blanket or what. I always write them out. Then I let the conversation flow in whatever direction it wants to go. Toward the end of the interview, I'll go back and glance through my notebook and make sure I haven't missed any questions, and generally I will not have missed any."

File Your Notes

After you write the story, number your notebook pages in sequence for each interview and write the date of the interview at the top of the first

research - public people
        private people
telephone interviews
tape recorder
conduct suggestions
        mistakes
bad questions
working with broadcast
group interview
ethical issues
how important - interviewing

This is a sample keyword list of questions about interviewing.

page. Staple the notes together and file them with the story file on the subject.

On a long interview project, reporters often keep their notes in their notebooks and number their notebooks in sequence. "Beachfront I," for instance, indicates that this notebook contains the first series of interviews on beachfront development that filled five notebooks. All the Beachfront notebooks can then be filed together when the project is complete.

Tape Recorders

Some reporters attach the same significance to their tape recorders as a carpenter would to a hammer—that without a tape recorder the job could not get done. Other reporters feel that a tape recorder stiffens an interviewee's answers or makes a reporter lazy and inattentive because the reporter stops listening.

Public Officials vs. Private Citizens

Generally, reporters who regularly interview *public officials* use tape recorders. "Most public people are so accustomed to tape recorders that they'd be almost surprised if you didn't use one," says Bill Endicott. "I'm always a little suspicious when someone agrees to an interview but doesn't want a tape recorder. The only thing that I can conclude from that is that he wants to be free later to deny anything he says. It's for their own protection as well as mine."

Even reporters who do not regularly use tape recorders admit they record conversations they feel may be challenged later, either by an editor or by the interviewee. A tape is a documented record. One reporter says he first decided to use a tape recorder when he matched his notes against a transcript of a governor's news conference he attended and realized what he had missed.

Every reporter, however, remembers a story about a time when the tape or the tape recorder didn't work. Bill Endicott had just interviewed a state senator. "I did an hour interview with him, I didn't take a single note, got back and found out the tape recorder hadn't worked.

"First, I sat down with a yellow legal pad and started madly scribbling all I could remember. Then I called him back. There were a couple of really good quotes that I desperately wanted. I said, 'I had a little problem with my tape recorder. It malfunctioned in a couple of places. Can I just ask you these questions again?' That is real panic, to take up an hour of somebody's time and realize that you don't have a damn thing. I didn't want to admit my stupidity."

For an interview with *private citizens* (people who suddenly become part of the news, such as a veteran who is awarded the Congressional Medal of Honor or a teacher who has just been named State Teacher of the Year), a tape recorder can be a significant barrier to a good interview.

"Put yourself in the interviewee's place," explains Kristin Gilger. "People are not afraid of giving you information. They are afraid of looking stupid. If you can make them feel you are sympathetic, they are going to talk more because they are less afraid of looking stupid." To help private people feel more comfortable, says Gilger, she usually uses only a notebook.

Tape Recording vs. Notetaking

Some reporters have such faith in electronic technology that their only record of what is said is on tape. In their notebooks, they jot down the counter numbers on the tape recorder to highlight a particularly useful comment, with a few words to indicate what was said. The notebook then becomes an index to the tape.

One hazard of this method is that, as Bill Endicott learned, the tape recorder may not work. Second, some reporters become so fascinated with counting numbers that they forget to listen to the interviewee. A third problem is that every quote you need is on tape, and you must review the tape before you can write the story.

Some large television news operations can do what they call "verbating," which means that someone transcribes the interview from the videotape verbatim before the reporter writes the story. But this is rare in most broadcast newsrooms, and nonexistent at newspapers. A reporter who tapes an interview and wants a word-for-word record must transcribe the interview. When you tape an interview, you have a complete record of what happened. But you also have a big obstacle. If you have two hours of tape, how will you find the appropriate 15 seconds quickly?

The best approach is to *simultaneously take notes whenever you use a tape recorder.* Rarely will you have time to transcribe an entire tape, but if you do, remember that each minute of taped conversation takes four minutes to transcribe. You will need at least four hours to transcribe a one-hour tape. An hour interview fills 20 double-spaced typed pages, which is much more information than you need for a quick story. So, when you takes notes *and* tape-record during an interview, use your notes as an index with the tape as a backup. You can write from your notes and use the tape only to check for specific quotes.

Cassette tapes record up to an hour on one side. Your interview could be 10 minutes on-the-spot or a reflective two-hour conversation. (A sit-down interview usually demands at least an hour.) When you decide which length of tape to use (30, 45 or 60 minutes on a side), overestimate the time you will need so that you won't have to turn over the tape in the middle of the interview. Carry extra cassettes as a backup.

Then check the tape before you start. Record the date, the story and the name of the person you are interviewing on the tape, then rewind it and play it back to make sure the tape is recording. This also gives you a good index to the tape's contents.

Most tape recorders work well with rechargeable batteries. A tape recorder without a cord is less obtrusive. You can simply set the recorder on the desk, press the record button, and begin the interview.

Rechargeable batteries run out after about two hours, however, so plug in your tape recorder whenever you can. Make sure that the plug you use is live and that the plug does not depend on a light switch to work. And always carry an extension cord in case the recorder's cord is too short to reach the electrical outlet.

Set the tape recorder between you and the interviewee, on a table or desk if possible. A hand-size tape recorder with a built-in microphone is less awkward than one with a remote microphone. (Remote microphones guarantee better-quality sound for broadcast interviews, however. Some remote microphones require a battery to work, so check that the battery is fresh.)

Also be careful of the "uh-huhs." Beginning reporters feel they must encourage their interviewee by nodding and "uh-huh-ing." This encouragement is good, but you will be surprised when you transcribe your tape at how many "uh-huhs" you managed to fit into one conversation. Broadcast reporters especially should avoid "uh-huh" altogether because one "uh-huh" in the middle of an audio or videotape can ruin the continuity of the recorded quote.

When the interview is over, label the tape's contents on the front of the cassette to file with your notes. You can listen to the interview and record your impressions while you are in your car returning from the interview to help you figure out the lead before you arrive in the newsroom.

Informed Consent

Whether an interview will be recorded is up to the interviewee. Most state laws require that you ask the interviewee's permission before you record an in-person interview, and the tape recorder should always be visible so there is no misunderstanding about whether the conversation is being recorded or not. Many attorneys advise that you mention something about the tape recorder to the interviewee while the tape is running ("Is this tape recorder in your way?") so you have a record of the person's knowledge that the conversation is being recorded.

The law is less clear on telephone interviews. Since an interviewee cannot watch the reporter or tape recorder during a telephone interview, some reporters record all telephone conversations, with or without the interviewee's knowledge, by tapping the microphone into the telephone outlet. These reporters claim they don't have to take so many notes, and they also are protected if people claim they have been misquoted.

Many states require that anyone who records a telephone conversation must inform the person who is being recorded, either verbally or by playing an intermittent beep tone during the conversation. A wise reporter treats a telephone conversation like an in-person interview and informs anyone being taped that the conversation is being recorded.

How to Use Your Notes to Write

To highlight your notes, use colored felt-tip pens. Circle important quotes with one color, important facts with another color. This will help you remember to include every essential piece of information in your story.

You also can use a yellow felt-tip highlight pen to mark important points and put circled code numbers next to important paragraphs. You can use ① for quotes, ② for facts, and ③ for background, for example. List the four or five quotes from your interview(s) that you feel should appear in your story, in the sequence that seems most logical. Then you can construct your story around the quotes, by adding facts and background. Or you can order the facts first and then fill in with quotes and background.

A Final Word

Notetaking is just one element of the interviewing process. The list of questions you prepare for your interview helps you focus the story before you face your interviewee. Once you've started the interview, the list you've prepared will help you handle any unexpected direction the interview might take. "I think the hardest thing about interviewing is that you have to listen very, very carefully, and you've got to be thinking about the next question at the same time," says George Curry. "You really have to listen and be prepared for the follow-up, make sure the person has answered your question and, at the same time, decide where you want to go next in the interview. That's the challenge of it all."

■■■■ A N   I N T E R V I E W I N G   C A S E   S T U D Y

Bill Endicott
The Sacramento Bee

Bill Endicott graduated from Transylvania University in Lexington, Kentucky. He worked for *The Courier-Journal, Tulare* (California) *Advance-Register, The Modesto Bee,* and *The Sacramento Union.* He was a reporter for the *Los Angeles Times* from 1968 to 1986 and is now State Capitol Bureau Chief for *The Sacramento Bee.*

When Bill Endicott wrote this story on Larry Mehau's involvement with organized crime in Hawaii, Endicott was San Francisco Bureau Chief for the *Los Angeles Times.* In this example, Bill Endicott was forced to rely solely on his memory of the interview because he couldn't do any notetaking until the interview was over.

"In the San Francisco bureau, part of our territory was Hawaii. We were doing a big piece on organized crime in Hawaii. There was a man who was purported to be a kind of godfather of organized crime in Hawaii. He had never been in jail, never been charged, never been convicted. On the surface, he was a respected man. But in street circles, his name constantly came up.

"I figured there was no way I could do that story without interviewing that man. He's a Samoan, a great big giant of a guy. I knew that I was going to have to try to interview him. He never talked to reporters.

"I knew that phoning him would never do any good. I knew where his office was, and I just drove over one morning and parked. This was going to be a hostile interview, I figured. This was going to be tough.

"He showed up with two huge bodyguards. He went into his office. I followed him. He was sitting in his outer office with a couple of guys. So I said, 'Mr. Mehau, I'm Bill Endicott from the *Los Angeles Times,* and I'd like to talk to you.' He said, 'Yeah, I heard you were in town. I'd like to talk to you, but I can't talk to you. My attorney doesn't want me to talk to anybody.' At this time he was under some kind of investigation.

"The trick that came to me was, 'How can I finesse this thing so I can talk to him and at least get a couple of quotes?' I didn't take out a notebook, didn't have a tape recorder. I just approached it as, 'Could we chat a few minutes? There have been a lot of rumors about you. If the rumors are false, we'll put them to rest.'

"He kept saying, 'I can't talk to you.' His attorney was there, and his attorney invited me to sit down. I knew I had made some inroads, at least, because I was invited to stay and I hadn't been beaten up yet.

"We chatted for about 15 minutes, then I left and got in the car and drove around the corner and got my notebook and started madly trying to reconstruct everything. I didn't really learn anything terribly profound from it, but I had at least given the guy an opportunity to have his say in the context of the story I was doing.

"The Hawaii papers picked up our story and ran it because they'd never been able to get an interview with the guy. Even though I didn't get any substantial information from him, at least it was evident that I had talked to Mehau, and I think it was important to do. I was at least able to say he'd been interviewed by the *Times*."

Hawaiians Stand in Awe of Ex-Policeman Who Some Believe Is Islands' "Godfather"

By William Endicott
Times Staff Writer

HONOLULU—Crime, organized and disorganized, is a preoccupation here. The newspapers are full of crime news. Everybody talks about crime. Gov. George R. Ariyoshi has said there is "an astounding and disheartening increase" in it.

The Hawaii Crime Commission, in a vaguely written report that contained no names, recently said the underworld has penetrated the highest levels of the state's political, social and entertainment circles.

It is a situation that lends itself to intrigues, mystery, partisan politics.

And it is a situation that demands a villain.

_____

Larry Ehukai Mehau, 49, is part-Hawaiian, a championship sumo wrestler, expert in karate and aikido, a friend and confidant of politicians, entertainers—and hoodlums.

His name is whispered on the streets and in the back alleys and bars of Honolulu with equal doses of respect, awe and fear.

Years ago, when he was a policeman, he reportedly put on a demonstration for some visiting police chiefs by suspending himself between two chairs and allowing other officers to hoist an 8-inch-thick rock onto his stomach and break it with a sledge hammer.

Mehau, so the story goes, didn't even grunt.

It is said here that his impressive physical prowess is matched by his political power, that he is the only man in Hawaii with unrestricted access to the governor.

And it is also said—and has been printed—that he is the "godfather" of the Hawaii underworld, the boss of the local crime syndicate.

The Honolulu office of the federal organized crime strike force has mobilized a grand jury to seek his indictment, reportedly on tax violations; the Hawaii Crime Commission keeps a file on him, and the local newspapers are probing contracts he has with state government.

"I wouldn't sanctify him too much," a source on the crime commission said to the Times when told the newspaper was preparing a story on Mehau.

But friends in high places continue to stoutly defend him; he continues to deny the allegations of crime links and so far, although it makes a good story, no one has publicly offered the barest shred of proof to support the godfather thesis.

A city of Honolulu prosecutor would talk only off the record about Mehau but then offered no substantive information, only rumor and street talk.

Still, the governor describes him as a "very close personal friend,"

entertainer Don Ho said he and Mehau are like brothers and attributed the godfather talk to "politics." Circuit Judge James S. Burns, son of the late Gov. John A. Burns, said Mehau is a "law-abiding citizen."

Burns said there is no doubt that Mehau knows people "who are and have been on the other side of the law. But nobody's ever proven a thing against that man. . . . I've kidded him about it, but I feel sorry for him."

For weeks, the Times tried to arrange a meeting with Mehau, but when an interview finally was scheduled, his attorney, Herbert T. Ikazaki, insisted that most of it be off the record because of the grand jury investigation and some other pending litigation.

That very day, Mehau had received a grand jury subpoena for his financial records.

"There's plenty I'd like to tell you," the 265-pound Mehau said. "I'm not a phony."

He conceded he knows "all the factions" in Hawaii's underworld through his years as a policeman. He said he has retained a network of informants, and because of a rapport with many of the state's toughest hoodlums, has been called on from time to time to help settle disputes between rival gangs, often at the request of the police.

After he left the police department in 1966, he said, "this damn guy," a fellow officer, began circulating rumors that "I'm the boss" of the underworld. "And that's how it started," he said. . . .

Entertainer Ho told the Times: "In my opinion, if it weren't for Larry there would be a lot of bloodshed in this town. A lot of bad people would have gotten away with things. He took a lot of bad boys and made them good boys and these guys are loyal to him to this day."

When a local union tried several years ago to organize workers at the famous Waialae Country Club in Honolulu, site of the Hawaiian Open, and threatened to send its goons to tear up the golf course, the club hired Mehau and his men.

"Larry has the capacity to go to these guys because he's as tough or tougher than all of them," a club member said. "And he knows them all and has done innumerable favors for a lot of these guys. They consider him someone they don't want to cross. . . ."

5

How to Get the Right Interview

Whether an interview lasts 15 minutes on the telephone or three hours in someone's home, you are using someone else's time and your own. Be selective. Before you begin an interview, be sure that the interview is the best way to get what you need. You must decide *who* will be your best interview and *why*.

The Interview WHO

People become part of the news for one or more of several reasons:

1. *Their jobs are important.* Public officials, corporation presidents, association and college presidents, even the bosses of organized crime, are recognized because of the positions they hold. Their job titles make them significant spokespeople for their professions and for the issues that affect their interests.

2. *They accomplish something important.* Celebrities and professional athletes achieve notoriety because the public enjoys and pays to see what they do.

3. *They are charged with an important crime.* A serial murderer who confesses to 35 murders from Maine to Arizona receives attention not because of who he is but because of what he did.

4. *They know something or someone important.* A secretary who saves incriminating memos that send the mayor to jail is momentarily

newsworthy. The companion of a movie star or a president often absorbs some of the radiated news glow because of the friendship.

5. *They have watched something important happen.* Witnesses to a crime or to a significant public event can give eyewitness information to embroider the event with specific detail.

6. *Something important has happened to them.* An accident victim, a plane crash survivor or a lottery winner fills a news interest because of the tragedy or the instant excitement of the event. Someone who receives an award, such as Teacher of the Year or Environmentalist of the Year, is newsworthy for the same reason.

7. *They represent an important national or international trend.* A traveler caught in the airport during an airplane strike, a young working couple who can't afford to buy a home, or a man who says he's exercising more because he's afraid of having a heart attack—each of these people represents a social or cultural change in the national or international community.

As an interviewer, you will want to talk to someone for one or more of these reasons. The categories often overlap, of course. Someone can be a celebrity and also a witness to an important event, or someone can be an important businessperson who receives an award, which means you will have even more to talk about. Deciding what makes the person newsworthy or noteworthy helps you focus the reason for the interview.

Public Figures and Private Citizens

The next distinction an interviewer must make is between interviewing public figures and interviewing private citizens. People who represent the first two categories on page 53 (people with important jobs, celebrities and professional athletes) are *public figures,* accustomed to being interviewed. People in the remaining five categories are usually *private citizens,* who often are unfamiliar with interviews and interviewers.

To *public figures,* members of the press are a predictable, everyday challenge that accompanies notoriety. "People being interviewed in public, or for use in public, are always very careful to protect themselves," says David Brinkley. "If there is anything damaging, they are not going to tell it. You get a very highly edited, highly colored, highly guarded view of whatever it is they're talking about."

Public officials relinquish their private lives to public scrutiny when they run for office. Corporate executives often learn to deal with the media as part of their training to become executives. Celebrities carefully feed the press to maintain celebrityhood.

Public figures and the press know how much they need each other. Public figures also understand the terminology (on the record, off the record) and the equipment (tape recorders, microphones and cameras).

"I always feel with politicians that they're never going to tell me anything they wouldn't tell 8,000 other people," says Susan Stamberg, "and I can't fault them for it. A slip of a word could cost them their jobs or a lot of votes. It makes them much more closed and much more guarded and, to me, much less interesting."

Private citizens usually are naive about how the media operate. Tragic or unexpected events can shove private people into the center of a bewildering circle of uninvited press attention. Private people usually offer a reporter few barriers, although they may be shy, suspicious or self-conscious at first.

The idea that someone else is interested in what they do, what they saw, or what they know often flatters private citizens, who are unaccustomed to the attention. "I think that, generally, people in trouble will talk," says former Canadian Press Wire Service Chief of Bureau Fred Chafe. "Maybe it's a release to them. Often you get a life story for an answer."

The Interview WHY

Whether you are interviewing a public or a private citizen, you should decide the purpose of the interview. What is your goal? Will you:

1. Gather facts?
2. Look for quotes?
3. Collect anecdotes?
4. Characterize a situation?
5. Confirm what you know?
6. Show that you were there?

To Gather Facts

To interview for an important fact, a reporter must find a verifiable, credible source with accurate information. If you ask a passerby for an opinion on the economy, you may have a good quote, but you do not have credibility. An economist obviously is more credible, even though economists often talk in jargon that you must translate. Your ideal interviewee on the economy, then, is someone who is not only quotable but also credible—an economist who can talk in an interesting way about a complex subject.

To Look for Quotes

Once you complete the factual research for a story, you must add interest. For example, you gather statistics about a new county program to give money to low-income people to help pay their winter electric bills. Then you interview a social worker, a utility company executive, and the mother in a low-income family to add personality. The story would be statistically accurate without the interviews, but your audience can see the statistics at work by listening to the people involved.

To Collect Anecdotes

Storytelling adds prisms of color and insight. A famous illustrator tells you that his first big job was drawing a cover for the *Saturday Evening Post* in 1940. But to enhance your profile, you include an anecdote: "I buried a picture of a nude in that cover illustration," the artist says, "and the stodgy *Post* almost decided not to give me another job. Then they got hundreds of letters from readers who had discovered the nude and praised the *Post* for its openmindedness. The *Post* decided to keep me."

To Characterize a Situation

The anecdote about the hidden nude characterizes the artist. You also can use someone's on-the-scene reactions to characterize a situation. You are sent to cover an earthquake, and an older woman is standing in front of the cement and wood shell of what was once her home. "Fifty years of my life is destroyed," she says. "In less than a minute, everything on the second story crashed through two floors to the basement." You can now portray the earthquake in a way your audience will remember.

To Confirm What You Know

Sometimes you need someone to verify or deny an accusation or some information that you have discovered. This may mean, for example, that you ask a utility company executive, "Why is this utility company interested in purchasing this specific piece of land?" and then follow up with what you know. "Is it because you personally own the property?" Interviewing for confirmation usually means that you know the answer to the question before you ask the question and that you are prepared to confront the interviewee with what you know.

To Show That You Were There

Reporters often show up at a story just because the newspaper or the broadcast station wants to show that it covered the story with its own reporter. "You often already know the answers you are going to get," says Bill Stall. "What you are looking for is a relatively short quote or two to show that you were there and to give added color."

Disasters and press conferences fall into this category. The news services will report the story, but individual reporters will still go to get a different angle. Be the reporter who finds a story that makes the trip worthwhile.

How to Select the Best Interviewee

Once you know *why* you want to interview someone—what they will add to the story—you are ready to choose just whom you will interview. People are useful as interviewees for one or more reasons: accessibility, reliability, accountability or quotability.

Accessibility

Can you easily get an interview with the person? If you can't, how long will it take? Will you meet your deadline if you wait? What barriers do you face in getting the interview? Can you write the story without the interviewee? If someone consents to talk, how long can the person give you? Can you conduct the interview by mail or by phone instead of in person? If the person is central to your story, be realistic about your prospects for the interview.

Reliability

Has this person been truthful before? Is the information independently verifiable as correct? Is the person a credentialed expert or an eyewitness? What motive does the person have for giving you the information? Remember that you will look pretty foolish if you report rumor or speculation from secondhand sources as fact.

Accountability

Is this person directly responsible for the information you want or for the actions you are investigating? Is there someone more accountable than this person for what occurred? How many people does a spokesperson represent? A spokesperson may speak for only a few people, and you won't know how many unless you ask.

Quotability

An expert who is articulate and well informed enhances a story just like an outspoken public official who likes to make controversial statements. Public figures usually know how to be quotable. They even can orchestrate quick quotes to satisfy reporters. Private people usually take longer to interview because they have not rehearsed their comments.

Sometimes the person you want to interview knows all the information, runs the operation, and speaks well but has left town for three weeks. Or you will find someone who is always available for a compelling quote but doesn't know what he's talking about.

The ideal interviewee, of course, is accessible, reliable, accountable and quotable. When an interview is significant to your story, look for an interviewee who combines all four of these characteristics.

Why People Refuse to Talk to You

Rarely do people say no to an interview. Instead, they say nothing—they don't answer the phone, they don't return your calls, or they tell a secretary to avoid you. Sometimes a journalist feels about as welcome as a cockroach. If you face a reluctant interviewee who is central to your story, you can:

- ■ Write the story without the interview.
- ■ Write the story stating that, after repeated attempts, the interviewee would not/did not answer your phone/mail/telegram/personal appeals to respond to your questions.
- ■ Convince the interviewee to talk.

A person who doesn't want to be interviewed might refuse an interview for any of these reasons:

1. *Time.* A potential interviewee who says, "I don't have time for an interview," wants to spend his or her time doing something other than being interviewed by you. The interviewee is computing the amount of time you will take and the advantages of being interviewed versus other uses of his or her time. Public figures will give this answer more than private citizens. Sometimes you are competing for a share of an already crowded day.

2. *Guilt.* Someone may be afraid that facing an interviewer will lead to an unexpected confession of wrongdoing. People understand the

dynamics of conversation enough to know that they may say something they didn't expect to say.

3. *Anxiety.* A shy person may be afraid of the actual experience of being interviewed. This uncertainty about the unknown can cause an interviewee to refuse to risk the new experience.

4. *Protection.* A person may be shielding a loved one or someone who is guilty of wrongdoing. An interviewee also may be afraid of being connected with an incident or a comment that will embarrass or condemn someone else.

5. *Ignorance.* An interviewee may not want to admit that he or she knows very little about the subject you want to discuss.

6. *Embarrassment.* A person may feel that the experience you want to discuss is humiliating, tasteless or too intimate.

7. *Tragedy.* A distraught person often does not want to share a personal catastrophe with the public. Adding a journalist changes the situation from a private to a public event.

How to Get the Interview

By Being Lucky

Sandra Thompson had been a reporter for Florida's *St. Petersburg Times* less than six months when she decided she wanted to do a telephone interview with Cary Grant. Grant was scheduled to appear in nearby Sarasota, so she called Grant's agent, who said, "Cary Grant doesn't give interviews, but I'll call him and ask." A few minutes later the agent called Thompson back and said, "If you call him in the next five minutes, he'll talk to you. Here's his number." Thompson interviewed Grant for half an hour.

By Focusing on What People Want to Talk About Rather Than What They Won't Discuss

"Another reporter and I did a series of stories on the Camanche Peak nuclear power plant, which is in Glen Rose, about 80 miles from here," says Doug Swanson of *The Dallas Morning News.*

"It's being built by Texas Utilities Electric Company, a big company here in town, and the government is saying the utility may not get a license to start up the $4 million power plant they had built.

"The Atomic Safety Licensing Board issued this memo to Texas Utilities that said, essentially, 'You are in big trouble.' I wanted to try to show how the utility reacted when that happened. The utility company executives were reluctant to talk about the internal workings of the company.

"So instead we began getting to know these people. We would say, 'Where were you when the news hit?' 'How did you get the news?' Some of them were on Christmas vacation. Some of them were at home watching their kids play soccer.

"We would ask them how they felt. Did they get a phone call? Did they get a letter or a telegram? Did someone stop by the house and tell them? Then we'd ask them what happened next. Did they come down to the office? Did they cancel their vacations?

"They were willing to talk about themselves individually, but not about the company as a whole. But by talking to enough executives and piecing together their reactions, in the end we painted a picture of this large, multi-billion dollar company going into a panic, with phone calls going out to these executives at home, men jumping into their cars and coming down to the company offices, going into this session to try to figure out what was going on."

By Filtering Through the Interference

When Joel Brinkley was a reporter for *The Courier-Journal,* he wanted to interview the president of Ralston Purina because Ralston Purina had spilled some toxic materials into the sewer, where the substance exploded.

The Courier-Journal sent Brinkley to St. Louis, Ralston Purina's headquarters, to do a profile of the company. "Of course you had to go through the public relations department," he says, "and the PR department didn't even tell the president I was interested.

"I decided I had to find some way to let the president know that I was interested. So I wrote a letter directly to him. I sent the letter ahead of the time I knew I was going for the appointment [with the PR person].

"I got there and asked the PR guy, 'Well, will the President talk to me?'

" 'No, I told you he won't,' the PR guy said. Then the phone rang and the PR guy said, 'Uh-huh, uh-huh, yes, sir.' There was a long pause and the president was reading the letter he had just that moment received. The PR guy said the president wanted to talk to me. [I took the phone] and the president said, 'I really admire your letter, and I think you're doing a wonderful thing. Come on up.' "

How to Handle Interference

Sometimes getting the interview means getting a chance to talk to the interviewee in the first place. A reporter who constantly deals with public figures faces many buffers—secretaries, attorneys, press secretaries and aides. These people can make an interviewer feel like a whining dog standing in front of a locked door.

A public figure or an executive can avoid an interviewer simply because someone else answers the phone. Some reporters, faced by a protective secretary or a reluctant aide, clutch the First Amendment to their chests and give a lecture about the public's right to know. You will be much more successful when you face someone who won't let you talk to an interviewee if you:

1. *Cultivate the person who shields the interviewee.* Be thoughtful, and try to remember the buffer person's first name. Often your courtesy transforms the buffer person into an advocate for the interview. The secretary or the aide may say to the interviewee, "I've talked to this reporter several times, and she's been very patient and polite. I think you should talk with her."

2. *Try to find a reason for the person to let you through.* For example, you can say, "I know everybody's calling you and you're about to go crazy. I'm sorry, but if you'll let me through, I won't bother you again."

3. *Call during lunch or after normal working hours.* Busy people often eat lunch at their desks and work long hours, including weekends.

4. *Ask for someone by a nickname or a first name.* "Is Pookie there?"

5. *Call the subject at home.* In casual conversation or through research, find out where your subject lives. A surprising number of public people are listed in the local phone book.

6. *Send a registered letter or a telegram.*

7. *Find the person in an informal situation* (in an elevator, at a parking garage, at a reception), *and ask for an interview.*

8. *Ask someone who knows the person to call or write a letter and vouch for you.*

Persuading Someone to Be Interviewed

Once an interviewee is talking to you, you should let the person know how important the interview is to your story. You put yourself in a difficult spot, however, if you try to get the interview by saying that what you write will be entirely flattering.

"I think it is a mistake to tell people that all you really want to do is a story about how wonderful they are," says Dean Bacquet. "That's dishonest.

Then you can't ask hard questions. Then it's hard to ask in the middle of the interview, 'So, is he a Mafia boss?' "

Instead, convince someone to talk to you by appealing to that person's:

1. *Sense of pride and fairness.* Explain that you will write the story anyway, whether the interviewee answers you or not. You will be forced to use the opposition's evidence without the interviewee's viewpoint. When people plead, "No comment," ask them to remember the last story they read about someone who said, "No comment." Did they think the person was guilty? Wouldn't they rather have an opportunity to explain their point of view?

2. *Instinct for justice.* Stress to the interviewee that information from the interview may help reform or protect a public policy or promote a public good.

3. *Need for attention.* Assure the interviewee that the public wants to know how he or she feels about this important subject.

4. *Ability to represent a point of view.* Emphasize that the interviewee is the best person to offer the most persuasive, most complete argument for his or her viewpoint.

5. *Sense of professional or personal prestige.* Point out the public significance that accompanies being quoted as an expert on a specific topic.

6. *Desire for community welfare.* Explain that other people in the same position will learn from the interviewee's experience.

Why Should People Talk to You?

A large part of a journalist's job is to convince people to talk. If you don't get the interview, you don't get a good story. So you must persuade an interviewee that talking to you is the best choice to make.

Start with Those Most Likely to Cooperate

Often an interviewee will ask, "Who else are you talking to?" Let people know that other people involved in the story agreed to be interviewed. When the U.S. embassy was bombed in Beirut, Lebanon, Joel Brinkley and Phil Taubman (at *The New York Times*) wanted to interview the ground commander. "Colonel Geraghty was being deluged with requests from reporters. He wouldn't talk to anybody.

"So finally we said [on the phone] to the PR guy, 'I think you ought to know that [Vice] Admiral Martin is talking to us, and he is Colonel Geraghty's direct superior, and we have appointments pending with General So-and-So and Admiral So-and-So. Don't you think Colonel Geraghty could talk to us, considering that his superiors are willing to talk with us about it?' There was a pause and the PR guy said, 'Hold the phone . . . What about 2 o'clock?' "

Negotiate for Time

If someone says he or she can't give you an hour for an interview, don't give up. Say, "How much time can you give me?" Once you are in the interview, you're likely to get more time than you scheduled.

Keep Talking

People who are reluctant to talk to you simply may need to hear your voice for a while on the phone to figure out whether they like you, whether they trust you. Be polite, but gauge the conversation to move the interviewee into your confidence. Sandra Thompson says Cary Grant "had a testy personality. So I was testy back. Soon he began to enjoy himself."

Be Sensitive

"If a woman's husband just murdered fifteen women and everybody in town is trying to talk to her, why should she talk to me?" says Maryln Schwartz. "I wouldn't talk to anybody. So that's what I tell her. I tell her I'm just as embarrassed as she is at having to go through this."

Give Hints About What You Know

Dean Bacquet says, "Give people a piece of information that shows that you have gotten into their realm." When he profiled underworld figure Carlos Marcello, Bacquet says that if he were trying to convince a Marcello friend to talk to him, he would "mention an anecdote, an intimate one.

"I would say, 'I have been told that you and Mr. Marcello loved hunting rabbits in the 1950s and had a really nice hunting lodge that nobody knew about with a fireplace and a red leather sofa.' First, it brings out a little bit of nostalgia. Second, it makes them think, 'This guy hasn't just talked to the Metropolitan Crime Commission and two FBI agents. This guy has talked to people who know what I know.' "

Show Up

Joel Brinkley used this tactic in Costa Rica, where rebels who were opposed to the Nicaraguan government paid bribes to Costa Rican officials so that the rebels could stay in Costa Rica. One government official had direct knowledge of how the bribes were being paid.

"My translator and I called him, and he kept putting us off and he was real gruff. So we got in the car and we just showed up at his house. We were nervous as hell. This guy had never been anything but gruff on the phone, and we were afraid he'd just slam the door. He was waiting at the door for us. He didn't want to say 'Yes.' On the other hand, he had information he wanted to get out, so [by showing up] we removed the necessity for him to make the decision to talk to us. He'd made coffee, and we talked for an hour and a half. It was wonderful."

Go Away for a While

"If somebody's reluctant to talk to you," says Dean Bacquet, "I can't think of any reason other than deadline to keep badgering them every day. That's just not going to work. Then they are going to have two reasons not to talk to you—the first reason is that they don't want to talk. The second reason is that they think you're a pain.

"If a person says, 'I don't want to talk to you,' then what I say is, 'Well, let me talk to some more people and get back to you in a couple of weeks.' Then I'll talk to some more people, maybe even ask some people who know the person to tell the person that I'm OK.

"People who are crucial interview subjects have a way of knowing that you're still working on the story. They're almost expecting you to call them back, and consequently they're still thinking about why you haven't called. Then I'll call the person again. If the person has weakened a little bit, then I try to convince the person to have a cup of coffee with me just to chat."

A Final Word

"I think you can talk just about anybody into talking if you remember to be truly concerned for them," says Maryln Schwartz. "People must start thinking about you as someone they trust before they want to talk to you. The really good reporters are just people you trust and you like, who treat you kindly."

AN INTERVIEWING CASE STUDY

George Curry
Chicago Tribune

George Curry is the New York City Bureau Chief of the *Chicago Tribune,* a job he assumed in 1989 after five years as a national correspondent in the *Tribune's* Washington, D.C., bureau. Before joining the *Tribune,* Curry worked for 11 years as a reporter for the *St. Louis Post-Dispatch* and two years as a reporter for *Sports Illustrated* in New York City.

Curry was asked by a new magazine, *Emerge,* to conduct an interview with the controversial leader of the Nation of Islam, Louis Farrakhan. After arranging the interview, Curry flew to Atlanta, where Farrakhan had given a speech to 19,000 people at the Omni International Center. The next morning, Curry interviewed Farrakhan in his hotel room. This interview shows how thorough research and careful questioning can prove rewarding for an interviewer.

"I had interviewed Farrakhan a lot in the past," says Curry. "I had access to him. People know nothing about his background. Some people see him as a dragon blowing fire. So I wanted an interview that would explain Louis Farrakhan as a person.

"The thing that helped me more than anything else with him is that he knows that I am fair to him. In the past, when there has been a controversy, I have called him for his comments. Part of his opening up to me was because of my past association with him. I had treated him fairly. My attitude is that you treat him like you treat anybody else.

"I had never read anything [published before] about his son being on crack. He didn't volunteer that; that was part of my preparation.

"When I prepared for the interview, I went back and looked at all the Muslim newspapers for the past two years, and there it was, right on the front page. Most people don't read the Muslim newspapers. So, the key to any interview, of course, is that you prepare yourself before you go there.

"Because he was coming off a whole round of TV interviews, I got transcripts of most of them. I got *The Washington Times* and *Washington Post* interviews that he had done. I had clipped *The Washington Post,* and I had somebody send me *The Washington Times.* I got the TV transcripts from a transcript service, and I went through my files on him.

"I suspect that he never would have volunteered that his son had been on drugs, but because I had done my research and asked him about [his son], it made him very candid. I had done my homework. It wasn't a matter of the great, perfect question. I had prepared for the interview, so I raised the question. I said that I had read about it in *The Final Call* [a Muslim newspaper].

"A lot of times in an interview it's not a matter of asking a question, it's just broaching a subject. It's not a matter of beating someone across the head. You come across as if you are holding a conversation and eliciting information.

"I am proud of getting information out of him that nobody else has gotten, from a person in public life for 30 years, and to humanize him and get him to talk about his fears. It made him a person. It doesn't mean you've got to like him. It's not my job to make someone like him. It's my job to make people understand him better. When you finish reading the interview, you should feel you know this person better. That's always the test."

Farrakhan, an Interview

By George E. Curry

Louis Farrakhan packed the house in April at the Omni International Center in Atlanta. Not counting the makeshift seats assembled on the floor, 19,000 people jammed the Omni. Instead of cheering for the usual talent, the Atlanta Hawks basketball team, this audience was screaming for Farrakhan, who was flying high after coming off a round of nationally televised interviews. A surprising number of those present were black teenagers born after three 1965 civil rights milestones—the Selma-to-Montgomery march, the passage of the Voting Rights Act and the bloody assassination of Malcolm X—and an equally surprising number were elected officials who were no longer offering excuses for having

to be "out of town" whenever Farrakhan was in town. . . .

Farrakhan ended his speech shortly before midnight, entertained friends in his three adjoining penthouse suites at a downtown Atlanta hotel until 3 A.M. and was up again at 7 A.M. for a long meeting with his ministers. Clearly exhausted, he wanted to postpone his 9 A.M. *Emerge* interview for later in the day, but at the urging of Akbar Muhammad, his longtime national assistant, he went ahead with it.

The two-hour interview provided a rare glimpse of Farrakhan's private side. Instead of the Muslim's trademark bow-tie attire, he was wearing a black jogging suit with blue and white stripes and a pair of black

Reeboks without socks. For the first time in anyone's recent memory, he did not have his own tape recorder running to guard against possible misquote; nor was his customary phalanx of bodyguards standing nearby. He sat at the head of a long table, and except for the interviewer, the only other person present was Akbar Muhammad, who had arranged the interview for *Emerge*. Farrakhan's voice was raspy as he sat sipping a cup of hot coffee, and his energy level seemed unusually low. But that was only until the interview started. . .

EMERGE: How many years had you been in the Nation before '84? That's when White America became acquainted with you.

FARRAKHAN: Approximately 29 years.

EMERGE: And they suddenly discovered Louis Farrakhan?

FARRAKHAN: As they suddenly discovered America with a house full of Indians. All these black artists that were on the chitlin' circuit, and then they discovered them. Until they discover us, we are not even in existence. What they are saying is that they are the light of their own world, and until we come into the light of their recognition we are not really in existence. And if you look into my history, I was never referred to as an anti-Semite until 1984. I was teaching 29 years, and the Jews knew what I was teaching because they were listening to me. It wasn't that I had not been on television before. I had been on television many, many times before, but I was never called anti-

Semitic until the Jesse Jackson campaign.

EMERGE: Why is that?

FARRAKHAN: Because I had never had an occasion to address the Jews. When Jesse decided to run, to give hope to a hopeless people, it was the Jews who came out with Jews Against Jesse [Jackson] and Ruin, Jesse, Ruin. All Farrakhan was trying to do was to get them to recognize that the way you handle Reverend Jackson, you are alienating this 90 percent of black people who are backing him. And at that point they called me a black Hitler. I took umbrage at that remark and defended myself. I called Hitler "wickedly great," and you know the rest. So I've been "anti-Semitic" ever since then. But I really don't care what they call me. I do care about what I am, because if a man is true to himself he will be true to everybody else. And I know that I'm not that [a black Hitler], so I really don't care what they say.

EMERGE: During Jesse's campaign, you became active politically for the first time?

FARRAKHAN: Yes, sir.

EMERGE: Why?

FARRAKHAN: The Reverend Jackson asked us to help him. I had no intention of becoming political. . . . For the first time we registered to vote, and I don't regret it. Because of the tremendous popularity that Allah, God, is giving me, I have the responsibility now to use that wisdom. I feel that a lot of politicians, black and white, don't represent the interests of black people. I want to use my popularity to get them out of city councils, state legislatures and Congress and put in those who will fight for justice for our people. And whether that politician is black or white, if that politician will stand up for justice for our black people, as the Honorable Elijah Muhammad said, we certainly will consider giving that politician our vote.

EMERGE: At one point I thought you were going to get out of politics altogether, after your experience with Jesse.

FARRAKHAN: At a point, I thought that would be the proper thing to do. I'm not a Democrat—I can't subscribe to the madness and the hypocrisy of the Democratic Party—and I'm certainly not a Republican. But I do recognize more and more the value of politics in aiding black people to get some measure of justice out of this society. So I'm beginning to feel more and more that we should use our strength politically.

EMERGE: Did you know in advance that Jesse was going to denounce some of your remarks?

FARRAKHAN: Denounce? No, sir.

EMERGE: You got no advance warning of that?

FARRAKHAN: No, sir.

EMERGE: How did you find out?

FARRAKHAN: Someone told me that they heard it on the radio or television, and I had not heard it. I was on my way to do an interview at CNN with Sandy Freeman, and I heard it over the news, that Jesse Jackson had repudiated Louis Farrakhan and that

my remarks—my alleged remarks— were morally reprehensible and indefensible.

EMERGE: You used the phrase "alleged remarks." Let's set the record straight. What was attributed to you that was not accurate?

FARRAKHAN: That I said Judaism is a gutter religion. I was speaking of the actions of the state of Israel— that their actions were in contravention of the religious teachings that they espouse. They are using God and religion as a shield for their unclean religion—parentheses—practices. . . . My explanation was never accepted. The press kept saying, whenever they mentioned my name, "Farrakhan, the man who called Judaism a gutter religion and called Hitler great." And this has dogged me for six years. . . .

In the January 15, 1989 edition of the Muslim newspaper the Final Call, *it was disclosed that one of Farrakhan's sons, Joshua, had been addicted to drugs and treated in Washington at the Nation of Islam's Abundant Life Clinic. In an interview with the paper's editor A. Wali Muhammad, Joshua said, " . . . the bottom line was that I felt that my father didn't care about his family, so why should I care about myself."*

EMERGE: I saw the *Final Call* in which you and your son were very candidly discussing how drug abuse had even reached your family. I presume that really caught you by surprise.

FARRAKHAN: Yeah. Unfortunately, some of us who work in the interest of our people are myopic sometimes in our view. We're going after the people, thinking that our families are all right, and we're not taking proper stock of those who are growing up right under our feet, so to speak. My son had been dabbling in drugs for a long time. I would hear it from people, and then I would ask him. He would always deny it. I told him, "Son, I can't help you unless you admit that this is what is happening." He said, "Well no, Dad. I used to do that, but I'm not doing that now." Of course, with most persons who use drugs there's a denial at first, particularly a denial to those whom they wish to have a good view of them. He continued until he got involved in crack cocaine, and it got so bad he just couldn't help himself. That's when we did our best to try and help him. So far he's struggling, but we see him turning the corner and overcoming it. He has become so wise in the recognition of this drug epidemic that I believe, as he gets completely pure of it and strengthened against it, he will be a great help to our young people and many of our families who have a member somewhere caught up in drugs.

6

How to Conduct an Interview

After you've looked through the clips, finished your research, uncovered all the documents, and found your interviewee, it's time to test your skill as an interviewer. The results (good or bad) of any interview depend on your preparation, organization, composure, poise, curiosity and on-the-spot wit.

Often out of insecurity, a new reporter tries to project the attitude that "I know it all. I've been here a thousand times before and you're not going to tell me anything I don't know already." This can be called the Rock Chewer School of Interviewing—"I'm so tough and I'm so mean that you should be afraid not only of me but of the entire American press establishment because we can hang you whenever we want." Rock chewers don't make good interviewers.

Good interviewers learn to relax their subjects so that the interview seems like a conversation instead of an inquisition.

■ "Never get too big for the person you're talking to," says Maryln Schwartz. "Some reporters get taken with being reporters. Even if you don't like somebody, you're going to have to try and understand them and give them every opportunity to tell what they're thinking and feeling.

"Some people want you to be tough," says Schwartz. "A scientist is going to expect you to know what the hell you're talking about. A doctor who doesn't have any time is not going to joke around. Socialites usually have a lot of time and need to be pampered. Big businessmen need to be flattered."

■ "I try to operate as though every step I take, every question I ask, every answer I get, every expression on my face is being covered on television," says Bill Nottingham, "and all the readers who eventually read my story are going to see exactly how I reported it."

■ "The key for me for an interview is to make it not seem like an interview," says Joel Brinkley. "There's always that notepad in your lap and you're always taking notes, but the interview questions should slide into what you hope is a natural and comfortable conversation."

■ "Being able to sit across the table, get the information you want and get a feel for the person is an art. Reporters really refine as an art the ability to gauge somebody," says Dean Bacquet.

Interviews can be informal or formal, on the telephone or in person, stand-up or sit-down. This chapter covers telephone interviews; formal, sit-down interviews; team interviews; group interviews; and press conferences. These suggestions will work for an interview on the run or on your feet.

How to Talk on the Telephone

When you were a toddler, your mother or father probably introduced you to the telephone by coaxing you to talk to a friend or a relative. Now you must learn to quickly befriend people on the telephone whom you may not know and may never meet.

"I do a lot of telephone interviews," says Sandra Thompson, "and what you have to do is create an atmosphere of intimacy with the person. It's not that easy, because obviously it's someone you've never met, you're talking on the telephone, you're in an office where there are phones ringing and typewriters going and you can hardly hear the person. I try to make the person feel like I'm calling an old friend for a long talk to find out what's going on." The ability to create instant intimacy is a skill nurtured by practice and experience.

Before You Begin

Prepare a list of five to 10 questions you would like to ask. This is important for in-person as well as telephone interviews, but telephone interviews often move faster, so you can easily overlook important information. During the conversation, you should add new questions as the conversation shifts and widens, but try to remember to write down the new questions, too. (Otherwise, you may find yourself afterward with a very definite NO! written in your notes, with no question to match.) Check off each question as you proceed, and then review the list before you hang up to make sure you have what you want. (For more information about notetaking, review Chapter 4.)

Your questions should be brief and direct, no longer than two sentences of 15 to 20 words. Complex questions are difficult for someone to understand over the telephone. If you have a complicated question, divide the question into several parts, and ask each part of the question separately in a logical progression of ideas so that your interviewee can follow you.

Diction is particularly important on the phone because you can overlook a crucial word. The difference between "do" and "do not" or "I am" and "I am not" is one word. Remember to speak slowly and deliberately, and restate the interviewee's answer if you have any doubt.

Also, whenever possible, learn the spelling of the person's name and exact title before the interview begins. Names are crucial in any interview— on the telephone or in person. Nothing demolishes a story's believability like a misspelled name or a mistaken title.

How to Begin

Always begin by clearly stating your name and your newspaper or broadcast station. When the news is moving fast, your voice can reflect your anxiety. Slow down your words, and use your voice to smile cordially. If the person who answers can't help, invite the person to help you find someone who can. When you need information quickly, explain that you're working on a deadline.

Once you reach the person you need, identify yourself again. Then ask, "Do you have time to answer a few questions now?" If the interviewee says no, then ask, "Do you have time to answer one question now?" If the interviewee still hesitates, ask when you can call back. Be prepared to give an estimate of how much time you will need to talk when you return the call.

If you have prepared questions for a news story on a deadline, be ready to ask questions as soon as the person answers the phone. Even if you're working quickly from very little knowledge, take any opportunity to ask questions even if you feel ignorant. You can say, "I'm new to this subject, and these questions may seem naive, so please be patient with me." An interviewer who is an eager student is usually irresistible.

For a long profile or a complicated factual interview on the phone, you often will get better results if you briefly explain to the person what you would like to talk about, and then offer to call back later. This gives the person time to gather documents and to organize statistics for each reference. For a profile, offer to call the person at home, away from work, where you will get more relaxed answers and where the person usually can give you more time. Then, remember the following suggestions:

Use the formalities. You may be tempted to call well-known personalities you do not know by their first names because they are familiar people. Instead, use a formal Mr., Miss, Mrs. or Ms. to address people you do not know until the person gives you permission to use a first name. If you do not know how someone prefers to be addressed, ask the secretary or press aide or ask the person directly before you begin the interview. The courtesy will be appreciated.

Set an agenda. Tell the interviewee generally why you want to know the information and what you want to know. ("I'm writing a profile of Mr. Walters at the Syntex Corporation [why] and I'd like to ask you about your friendship with him [what].") This focuses the interview and gives you and the interviewee a sense of shared purpose.

Develop a partnership. A shared goal is important in any interview, but especially in telephone interviews, says Bill Nottingham. "I try to bring the person I'm talking to in as a partner on the story." Nottingham says the best approach to an interviewee is, "You can help me a lot if you'll give me accurate information," and "You don't want me to write an inaccurate story, do you? Let's work together." He says he tries to make the interviewee feel, "This is a newspaper reporter and me, trying to get the facts out."

Clarify jargon and spelling. Circle any confusing jargon, dates and names in your notes, and come back later for clarification, unless the terms are essential to understand as you go. An interrupted sentence detracts from the conversational flow. If a thought is unclear or you get behind in your notetaking, wait until the interviewee finishes a sentence and then say, "Are you saying that . . . ?" or "I'm not sure I understand. Could you please explain that again?" This will give you time to catch up.

Keep talking.   Few people will hang up on someone who is talking. If you need the story quickly but you sense someone is uncomfortable or in a hurry, you can say, "I have just one more question," even though you have four more. Interviewees may get impatient with your persistence, but they rarely hang up. If the person insists on ending the conversation, ask when you can call back to finish the interview.

Prepare for "no comment."   People who don't want to answer a question on the telephone can make a special exit—they can hang up. So you must be especially persuasive with a reluctant telephone interviewee. Bill Nottingham clearly explains the consequences of a "no comment" answer. He tells the interviewee, "If I don't have this information in my story, it's because you didn't want to give it to me. And I'm happy to say that in my story. I'm happy to say that I called you up, Mr. Official, and you didn't want to comment. And everybody who reads the story is going to know that you could have commented if you wanted to." He says this usually persuades the interviewee to answer.

Don't waste time with people who won't talk.   If someone absolutely doesn't want to talk to you and the person is secondary to your story, find another source. "You learn that certain people aren't talkers or certain people will never trust you or they hate the press," says police reporter Walt Philbin. "I don't waste time trying to use techniques to interview them. I use people who are talkers."

Nottingham explains, "I exude straightforward dedication to the story, which says, 'I would very much like your help, but if for some reason you can't help me, thanks very much. I'll go find someone who can.'"

Conclude the interview.   Always ask for daytime and nighttime phone numbers and an address. Also find out whether the person will be available later. Ask the interviewee for permission to call back for more help, if necessary. Repeat your name and give your phone numbers so that the person can call you with any new information. Be sure to say, "Thank you."

Remember a phone interview's limitations.   A phone interview is good for quick, direct answers on a deadline. But Daphne Bramham says she is very conscious of the phone's limitations. "In a telephone interview, what you get is the answer to the question you phoned to ask. If you go in person, there's a good chance you'll get the answer to the question you asked and four different story ideas. Lots of times, the question that you go to ask is even less important than the leads you get."

How to Prepare for a Formal Interview

A formal interview begins as soon as you make the appointment. Prepare a list of questions you want to ask. Read through your research to make sure you haven't overlooked an important point. Seven good questions and answers will fill an hour. Don't arrive for an hour interview with 25 questions (see Chapters 4 and 7). Be familiar with the questions, but do not memorize them so literally that you are closed to new ideas or new information.

Location

The interviewee usually determines where an interview will occur, but if the interviewee expresses no preference, choose an informal spot over a formal location. A businessperson feels formal in the office, less formal at home. A professional athlete's office is a track or a playing field, so visit the athlete somewhere else. A university scientist who works in a laboratory may feel more relaxed in the campus park. For a detailed profile, you may want to interview the subject both at work and at home to see the parallels between the person's professional and personal behavior.

For interviews with private citizens, especially on a breaking story, do your interviews on the scene whenever possible. You can even return with the interviewee to the site of an event, such as the street where a robbery took place or the stadium where an athlete won a medal. You will get a better interview because the site is a reminder of the event.

Distractions

Telephones, secretaries and visitors interrupt an interviewee's thoughts and yours. Try to take someone away from as many distractions as possible. An interview on an airplane or in the back seat of an automobile can be surprisingly intimate because there are so few distractions. An interview in a restaurant competes with the waiters, the children throwing food at the next table, and the salad dressing that you've just spilled on your pants.

Try to keep the interview a twosome. For print interviews that need pictures, try to schedule the photo session separately from the interview because the photographer's gymnastics may fascinate your interviewee more than you do. Your goal should be uninterrupted time for both of you to talk. (To learn how to handle group interviews, see pp. 84–86.)

Time

When you make the interview appointment, be realistic about how much time you will need, especially with a public figure who carefully allocates each appointment. If you are doing several consecutive interviews, schedule some extra time between them to allow you to stay with a good interviewee longer than you planned. Also, never begin an interview by setting a deadline to end it. You and your interviewee will consciously and subconsciously abbreviate comments. What you want instead are relaxed answers.

An unconventional time for an interview also can be an asset. Police officers are used to talking with reporters during the day, but at night the atmosphere is different, says police reporter Walt Philbin. "I like off-hours reporting," he says. "I find that when you interview cops and establishment people late at night, at 1 or 2 o'clock in the morning, there's a certain camaraderie. Their boss is home asleep."

Also be sensitive to someone's fatigue. When the answers begin to repeat or the person begins to move uncomfortably in the chair or changes position often, the interviewee is weary. You rarely will get good new information if you force the interview beyond this point.

If you must complete the interview that day because of your deadline, find an excuse to get up and stretch—use the telephone or ask for a short tour of the building, for example. If you don't face an imminent deadline, and someone seems too tired to continue after a brief break, offer to return on another day to finish up.

Silent Conversation

Conversation in any interview occurs on two levels—silent and spoken. The silent conversation in an interview begins before you ask any questions. When you arrive promptly, you are saying, "I know your time is important. So is mine." When you smile and reach out to shake hands, you are saying, "I'm a friendly person who is interested in you." When you accept a cup of tea or coffee, you are saying, "I'm grateful for your cordiality."

June Kronholz says tea plays a particularly important role in the Third World. "Third World people—Indians, Pakistanis, Asians, Africans—set much store by hospitality, and tea is part of that. I was in Amritsar, India, in the Holy Temple, the most sacred shrine of the Sikhs, interviewing Longowal, a Sikh 'sant,' or priest. Naturally, he offered tea.

"For once, I asked that mine be served the way I prefer it—black, without sugar. The sant was dismayed: How could he show hospitality if I refused his milk and sugar? The matter was debated at length, and finally he agreed that the tea would be sugarless and black.

"So as not to enjoy any delicacies that his guest wasn't enjoying, he announced he'd have his tea black, too. To show hospitality—to make up for the lost sugar and milk—he ordered the tea brewed twice as strong.

"I couldn't drink it, he couldn't drink it, and the interview was awful. A lesson there is: Put your subject at ease, and you will come away with a better interview."

The way you dress can be another signal to an interviewee. Dress as you expect the interviewee to be dressed. "Don't make your interviewee uncomfortable because of your dress or actions," says Tommy Miller of the *Houston Chronicle.* "If you have an appointment with [former Texas Governor] John Connally to interview him in his Houston law office, don't wear your jeans and boots," says Miller. "Put on your Sunday duds. Look sharp. By contrast, if you go out to the rice farms near Winnie, Texas, to interview a farmer out in the country, don't put on your best three-piece suit and Christian Dior tie. That garb will scare the hell out of him, or he may fall over laughing. Blend in a bit."

For Bill Nottingham, one answer was a mustache. "When I moved onto the police beat, I never thought the police were really taking me seriously, so I grew a mustache. A year or two later, when I was covering grand juries in the federal courthouse, I found out that you get a marvelous amount of information if you just wear a three-piece suit and stand in the halls as though you know something. People will talk to you. They think you're a lawyer. I never represented myself as a lawyer, but anything that will put the subject at ease, I'm happy to do."

How and where you sit also are important. Try to lure your interviewee out from behind any barriers, such as a desk or a large table, which acts like a barricade to candid conversation. If you're too tall or too short for your interviewee, do the interview sitting down. Sit where you can look comfortably into someone's eyes, and lean forward into the conversation to encourage intimacy.

Where Do You Start?

At the beginning of an interview, a person wants to hear your voice and get a chance to decide whether you're likable and trustworthy. Be prepared for a few minutes of casual introductory conversation. "It's a good idea to know some nice little details about your subject before you go in," says Dean Bacquet. "That little tidbit gives you something to use to start the conversation. For example, if I'm going to interview a lawyer, I try to know his last big case.

"I almost want to let the interview subject let the introductory banter end," says Bacquet. "I don't want to be the one to say, 'Let's get down to business.' I like to let the person talk out the introductory conversation until eventually there is a long silence. The subject is saying, 'OK, I'm comfortable. I'm warmed up. Let's go.' And then the reporter takes over the silence."

Set an Agenda

Once you feel your interviewee is comfortable and ready to talk, you are responsible for the success of the interview. Just as in a telephone interview, you should tell the subject how you plan to spend the time you have requested. In two or three sentences, explain the focus of your story (see "Set an agenda" on p. 73).

During the Interview

Once you set an agenda, you are ready to ask your first question. This question sets the tone for the interview—establishes your knowledge, your insight, your purpose. You also are warming up the interviewee. Few people can give you articulate prose immediately.

The first question should be interested and informed, but not trite. Historical questions often are a good beginning—"I read once that you said . . ." or "Can you tell me what personal experiences led you to feel the way you do about this issue?"

For celebrities and public figures especially, the first question should be new—an angle you have never seen in your research about the person. Practiced interviewees appreciate the opportunity to say something new, and you are communicating to them that you are well prepared.

Save uncomfortable or accusatory questions for the last third of the interview. If you ask a difficult question first, you may be out in the street before the second question (see Chapter 7).

After two or three questions, the interview should begin to glide. Remember the following suggestions:

Relax

Let the interviewee talk. Sometimes you must listen to information that is unimportant to your story, but the purpose is to relieve any tension that still exists. "If somebody is talking about something that's really not important to your story, you still are getting them used to you taking notes, doing reporterlike things, before you get to the sensitive areas," says Bacquet.

"If the person you're interviewing decides to tell you 10 stories about rabbit hunting and you have the time, you should just listen, and try to gently steer back to the issue. To get six paragraphs of very crucial profile information, you may have to listen to an hour about rabbit hunting."

Display Empathy and Concentration

Steal some ideas from professional counselors. Face people squarely and look them in the eyes. Try to keep your legs from moving too much so that you seem relaxed. (Have you ever watched someone cross one leg over the other and draw circles in the air with their extended foot while you're trying to talk?) Move comfortably close the person. Nod and smile when appropriate. Be solicitous but not deferential.

Note Gestures, Nuances, Expressions

Does the movie star condescend to her manager-husband? Does the executive seem proud of his indoor plants? Does someone fidget or sit inert, hands and legs crossed? Does an unanswered phone make the person nervous? Does the tennis star unconsciously grab and begin to pluck the strings of her racket while you talk?

Note Physical Characteristics

You will forget someone's less-than-memorable brown eyes, but you may need the detail later for your story. Especially for a profile, write down your impression of height, weight, build, posture, complexion, eye and hair color. What colors is the interviewee wearing? Does the person have freckles? Pimples? Freckles and pimples? Does the person wear jewelry—four earrings, two earrings or one?

Look Around

Does the interviewee display awards on the wall? Are you in a room full of antique, traditional or modern furniture? Is a St. Bernard licking your ankles? Is there an exercise machine in the corner? Is the person wearing sandals with a suit? You may need these descriptive nuggets to write the story.

Listen as You Go

Be alert for the significant quote or anecdote, and underline or star the comment in your notes. This will save time later. Listen for your lead, the main thrust of the story, as the person talks. A good reporter will silently write and revise the lead as the interview progresses.

Be Quiet

"I find it frustrating to be in that very passive role of interviewer," says Sandra Thompson. "I'm always cutting myself off from saying things I want to say." Thompson has learned that people do not consent to interviews so that they can listen to a reporter talk. You are a chatterbox if you talk more than 10 percent of the time. "A lot of reporters talk too much," says Dean Bacquet. "A conversation, a give-and-take, is fine. But you can't quote yourself."

Be Alert for Shifts in Conversation

Almost every interview reveals new information, but always listen for a new angle that makes your story better. "I was writing a column on the fire department's fund drive," says Kristin Gilger. "I talked to the mayor and asked whether he thought we needed better fire protection services. After about 15 minutes, he told me he was going to propose a sales tax for fire protection. I didn't know that and no other reporter did, either. I found out just because I spent the time talking to him. The whole interview lasted about 25 minutes."

Be Willing to Show Your Ignorance

"The key mistake reporters make, I fight against it all the time," says Joel Brinkley, "is being more concerned about the impression they're giving the other person about themselves. Reporters are often more worried about making someone like them and being impressive than in getting the information.

"To counteract that, I will, at the outset, tell people, 'You're going to be asked some really naive questions. I'm a beginner at this subject, and I hope you will excuse the naivete of my questions.' Then if you end up asking some questions that are a little more sophisticated than they had expected, they like it. They like taking the role of a teacher."

Avoid Arrogance

"The grizzled veterans seem to try to convince the person that they are questioning that they know more about the issue than the person they're interviewing," says Doug Dowie. "You end up with a debate on some esoteric subject that never appears in the story."

Be Selectively Silent

An unfilled silence gives an interviewee time to collect new thoughts or to expand on an idea. Toward the end of an interview, try pausing for a few seconds after someone's response before asking the next question. This reflective perspective may surprise you.

Ending the Interview

Interviewees expect you to conclude the interview. Courteous people will try to answer you as long as you keep asking questions. When you are nearly ready to end the conversation, you can say, "I have just a few more questions," which signals that this is the last chance someone will have to say what he or she wants. Often interviewees will talk longer after this warning because they think this is their last opportunity to say something important.

Summarize the Conversation

Rephrase what you think was said overall, and ask the source to elaborate if he or she disagrees with your summary. Then, as a protection against later criticism from the interviewee that you overlooked something important, ask the person, "Have I overlooked anything you would like to add?" and, finally, "Is there anything I've forgotten to ask?" Many people wait for this opportunity to give you the information they feel is most important.

Don't End the Interview Prematurely

As you ask your last question, don't be so anxious to leave that you overlook new information that can still change your story. One journalist was interviewing a well-known artist. While the reporter was gathering up her tape recorder and notebook, she asked one last question as an afterthought. "Where did you learn your technique?" "Oh," said the interviewee, "while I was an American prisoner in a Japanese prisoner-of-war camp during World War II." Quickly she set down her briefcase and began a second interview.

Put Away Your Notebook but Keep Listening

As you stand up and walk toward the door alongside the interviewee, you are usually physically closer to the person than at any time during the interview. This often elicits unexpected confidences. Keep listening, and be ready to recreate the conversation in your notebook as soon as the door closes.

Prepare the Person for a Call Back

To let someone know that you will check any unclear details later, say, "Would you mind if I called you back with any further questions?" Also give the person your phone number, and encourage the person to phone you with any new information.

Deny Requests to Preview the Story

A common misconception among many interviewees is that they will be able to check what they have said before it's in print. Assure the interviewee that you will call to check any unclear technical or statistical information. If you are a print reporter, convince the person that you understand the difference between the spoken and the written word and that you will clean up the syntax and grammar (except, of course, if their use of language is part of the story—see p. 141). Offer to provide a copy of the story *after* it appears, but never before.

Say "Thank You"

Some reporters forget this simple courtesy, but remember that you may need this person for information again. With a firm handshake and a direct look in the eye, always show your gratitude for the time someone is willing to give you. If someone has been particularly gracious and helpful or has spent an unusual amount of time with you, write a thank you note recognizing the person's contribution to your story. This can distinguish you from other reporters and may help build a good relationship for possible future contacts.

Five Special Interview Situations

The age of your interviewee and the number of people involved in an interview deserve separate discussion because they provide special challenges. Children can be very forthcoming, but the accuracy of the information they give you can be influenced by many factors. In team interviews or when you interview a group, the number of people changes, and the reporter should learn how to benefit from the change. In other cases (with a press aide or third person present or in a press conference), the reporter must negotiate for the interviewee's attention.

Interviewing Children

Children deserve special caution as interview subjects because they are more vulnerable than adults. As an interviewer, you have a special responsibility to protect the child's vulnerability yet still get the story.

Except at a news event, interviewing children requires the permission of a responsible adult. Photographing children also requires adult approval.

When you interview a child, the first thing to do is to sit down. This puts the two of you closer to eye level and removes the intimidation of adult size.

Then, remember the following cautions. For a favorable feature story (spelling bee winners or scholarship recipients, for example), these warnings will not be as important as when children become part of a news event. Children who become part of a crime (murder, child abuse or robbery, for example) or an accident (bus crash or drowning, for example) require special treatment.

Ask open-ended questions. Remember that most children want to please adults. Children will say what they think you want to hear. Be very careful not to lead children during an interview. By asking open-ended questions ("What happened?" "Can you describe what you saw?"), you will be more likely to elicit accurate information.

Independently verify what children tell you. Many children cannot easily separate fantasy from reality. As adults, we treasure this aspect of childhood, but as an interviewer, you should not use children as your only source of information.

Ask the same question several times. Interview the child using a short list of questions, and then go through your list again. If possible, return several hours later or the next day and run through the same list to see if the child gives you the same answers. Information that remains the same through several sessions is more likely to be accurate.

Interview each child privately. Children can be impressionable and, when interviewed in a group, often listen to their friends and then repeat their friends' stories as if the stories were their own. Separating the child from other children helps remove this hazard.

Be sensitive. The emotional trauma associated with a criminal or accidental event touches a child deeply. Do not add to that trauma by badgering a child for information.

Team Interviews

To cover a particularly wily interviewee or an extremely intricate issue, some journalists team up in a two-on-one interview. At the *Los Angeles Times,* Bill Stall joined fellow reporter W. B. Rood to interview Congressman B. F. (Bernie) Sisk. Sisk and two other congressmen controlled California's $3.7-billion, 400-mile federal water system, and the story showed how the three congressmen negotiated in Congress for California agriculture.

"Two people conducting an interview is a real asset," says Stall. "You can think ahead while the partner is asking questions. Afterward, you can discuss the interview. Sometimes you are so intent on asking all the questions that it is easy not to pick up on something someone said."

Interviewing a Group

"If you are talking to people about things they don't want to talk about, things that are unflattering, try like hell not to have the interview in a group," says Joel Brinkley. "Everybody's real resistant to say anything because they know everybody else is listening. When I was in Beirut to interview the staff of the American Embassy about the role of the State Department in the bombing of the embassy, we arrived at the ambassador's residence, and almost the entire staff was there. They were all wearing suits, and these people were serving little cheese sandwiches with triangle napkins with the State Department seal on them. Suddenly it was a big, official thing, and none of the people said a word."

For another Brinkley assignment, however, a group interview improved the story. He was reporting how Kentucky state laws were inadequate to protect nursing home patients. Several nursing home inspectors gathered in a room around a table. "They had never talked to the press before. Their boss was at the head of the table. I thought, 'This is going to be a disaster.'

"Then the boss told an anecdote and some people [figured out] it was OK to talk. Then suddenly it started just a flood. These people had been upset and frustrated about nursing home enforcement for a decade, and nobody ever paid any attention. One story would prompt another story about patients who would get hurt or killed because of the inadequacy of the state law.

"If you're talking to a group of people who all have a shared experience that they want to talk about, groups work wonderfully. They all reinforce each other. If you talk to them by themselves, you don't get this group dynamic."

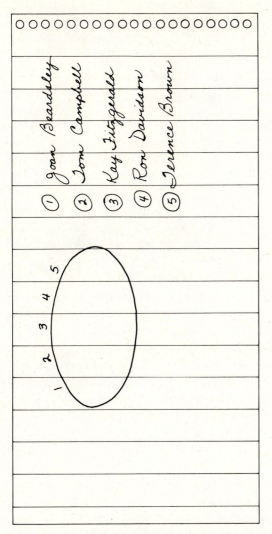

Use a numbered diagram to identify people in a group interview.

When you do interview a group, use a numbering system to identify members of the group. Draw a diagram of the seating arrangement, and fill in each person's name on the diagram before you begin. Check spelling and titles. Then assign each person a number. Leave the diagram in front of you when the interview begins. In your notes, you can connect each person's comments to a number instead of writing down the person's name each time.

Former *Newsday* reporter Stuart Dim, who suggests this numbering system, says that in group interviews, "sometimes it becomes obvious that only a few in the group have something interesting to say. Zero in on them—they have the story you want."

Interviews with a Press Aide Present

Some public officials feel uncomfortable without an aide standing by. To an interviewer, this can be an asset and a liability. The aide can be an asset if he or she can selectively add detail that the interviewee forgets. The aide can be a liability if he or she interrupts or becomes the focus of the interview instead of the interviewee.

In China, says June Kronholz, one interview attracted quite a crowd. "I was in Wuhan, China, reporting a story on China's urban policies. I felt very lucky to be granted an interview with the mayor. I arrived with my interpreter, who was traveling from Peking with me, and with a local guide and interpreter assigned us by the foreign ministry.

"The mayor brought his PR woman, a couple of aides and his own interpreter. There were 11 of us sitting on the upholstered sofas and divans that lined two long walls of a huge reception room. We talked for an hour, and we all took notes. The mayor's interpreter took them in triplicate."

To avoid problems in a situation where you know a third person (or a crowd) will sit in on the interview, establish the rules beforehand. Explain that you are glad to have help, but that everyone should remember that the interviewee is the focus of the conversation. If someone can help you substantially, you will ask for that information when the interview is over. But you would appreciate as much uninterrupted time with the interviewee as possible.

"By the way I sit," says Joel Brinkley, "looking at the interviewee, not at the aide, I try to cut the other person out of the conversation." Brinkley says every Pentagon interview involves a third person, who tape-records the conversation along with the reporter.

Once Brinkley used this habit to his advantage. "I remember I interviewed a general, and he had said all these wonderful quotes that I didn't have time to write down. I just called the Pentagon and said, 'Can I borrow your tape?' And I used the Pentagon's tape to quote the general."

Press Conferences

In a press conference, a reporter surrenders command to the interviewee. A reporter has less control in a press conference than in any other interviewing situation.

The location and time are decided by the interviewee. The content of the conference is also largely decided by the interviewee. The length of the questions, the number of questions, the order of the questions, and even who will ask the questions are the interviewee's decisions. The positioning of the cameras and the location of the reporters are organized by the interviewee.

The confusion of a crowded press conference also gives the advantage to the presenter. Jockeying for space and advantage, reporters look like a group of hyperactive children. What comes out of a press conference is usually what the interviewee wants to come out.

A press conference is, by definition, the official word. The official word is necessary, and occasionally the press coaxes new, surprising or spontaneous comments from someone. But the best advice for a reporter is to cover the press conference, use the information as background, and then work to get more than the official word.

Broadcast and print reporters simultaneously cooperate and compete at a press conference. "It's my reporter's job, and it was my job when I was a reporter, to come back with the story I was sent to get," says former Managing Editor Doug Dowie. "If there are two dozen television cameras, jockeying for the best position, which is up front, and they're going to put you in a position where you're going to be pushed back, you simply get up in front and you sit down. You don't move. You are no good to me if you call me and say, 'I didn't hear anything because all the television cameras were in front of me.' "

At a press conference, broadcast and print reporters both tolerate and use each other. Broadcast reporters often use the answer to a print reporter's question with the introduction, "So-and-so was asked . . . " Print reporters listen to a broadcaster's questions, and use the information to develop better questions for a private interview afterward.

Reporters develop different tactics to be sure they are recognized at a press conference. Even though the White House press conferences follow a prescribed format, ABC's Sam Donaldson says, "Presidents, like most politicians I know, call on people who are interesting. We like interesting people, whether we're going to have them over to dinner tonight, or whether we're at a news conference and we're going to call on someone to question us. We don't like dull people."

Print reporters also know that a camera encourages showboats to talk. "If someone is enjoying attention of the TV cameras," says Doug Swanson, "I'll stand right beside the camera and make sure that I'm part of the whole show. I bask in the reflected glory of the TV camera."

One reporter says that, if he knows someone wants to avoid him in the hallway after a press conference, he asks his television friends to hold up a camera and turn on the lights as the person passes. The interviewee thinks the cameras are running, and the interviewee talks.

Bill Endicott, who covered three presidential campaigns, says, "Campaigns have just become one gigantic photo opportunity. The print media are along as bit players, and the importance that I think is frequently attached to what we do is that we set the agenda for television. Much of the television coverage flows from what television reporters read in the newspapers."

To take the best advantage of a press conference:

1. Whenever possible, do research before the press conference that will take the story beyond the official handouts.

2. When you arrive, make sure you can see and hear.

3. Don't ask a yes-or-no question because there probably will be no chance for a follow-up.

4. Realize that if you ask your best question in a press conference, everyone else will get your story.

5. Decide where you will get your best chance for worthwhile answers—here or in a separate interview later. If this is your only chance for a story, ask your questions; otherwise, wait.

6. Particularly in a press conference, make your questions succinct.

7. Listen to everyone else's questions as well as your own.

8. If you don't understand something, ask about it. In a group, many reporters are too timid, and they are afraid of looking stupid. If you are confused, you will write a confusing story.

9. Recognize the dynamics of working around other reporters. Don't adopt every other reporter's idea of the story. Think independently.

10. Whenever possible, get your own quotes before or after the press conference.

11. Understand that the story is probably *not* at the press conference. Press conferences are one-dimensional. Use the press conference as background for a story with perspective.

A Final Word

The best way to conduct an interview is to make people want to talk to you—for whatever reason. The suggestions in this chapter about how to conduct yourself are not precise prescriptions. Adapt your own personality and your own judgment to each situation. And remember that a good interviewer should be sensitive yet observant, critical yet open-minded.

■ AN INTERVIEWING CASE STUDY

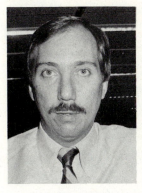

Bill Nottingham
Los Angeles Times

Bill Nottingham worked for the *St. Petersburg Times* after he graduated from the University of South Florida in 1973. With two other reporters, Nottingham spent nearly a year covering the University of Florida athletic program, an assignment that produced more than 30 stories, which he says were "perhaps the most controversial thing I've ever done." In 1984, the Associated Press Sports Editors Association awarded the series first place in investigative reporting. Nottingham is now an assistant city editor at the *Los Angeles Times*.

For this story about a University of Florida defensive lineman who received a passing grade on the eve of the big football game for a class he never attended, Bill Nottingham wanted printed verification of the grade. In this difficult interviewing situation, notice how Nottingham persuaded an interviewee in a telephone interview to provide information that was crucial to the story.

"I came upon a university professor. Federal law says that [a university professor] can't give out academic information about a student. So I started by asking some general questions about coursework.

"Pretty soon I was saying, 'Well, what quarter did he attend that class?' And he said, 'Well, it says here in my file that . . . ' He had started to read something over the phone. I was inching closer and closer to the information I needed. Suddenly the person on the other end of the phone said, 'Oh oh, I just realized what you're heading for here. I realize that I have put my foot in it.' And I said, 'I sure wish I had a copy of that.' And he immediately realized what was going on.

"At that point it becomes tough reporter time. 'Look, Mr. —————, you're a nice guy and I've enjoyed this conversation if it ends now. I appreciate all your help. But here's where we've got to be partners in this interview. I don't mind telling you that we've been talking on the record, and this is going to have to go in the newspaper.'

"He said, 'Oh, my job. I'll lose my job.' So I said, 'All I want to know is that what you're holding in your hand is legitimate. I don't need to ruin your life, and I don't want to.'

"So in the mail I received, without knowing from where it came, this memo that we produced in the newspaper. The memo said that, according to a university official, this football player attended this class and received a grade of satisfactory, one day before the opening game. We had already interviewed the player and found that he did not attend, so we had the story locked."

Gator Player Says He Didn't Attend Class That Saved Eligibility

By William Nottingham, Dave Scheiber and Robert Hooker
St. Petersburg Times Staff Writers

A University of Florida athletic official saved a football player from becoming ineligible for the 1981 season by giving him credit for a class the player says he never attended.

Assistant Athletic Director H. Wright Waters, the official involved, was able to award the additional credit because he doubled as the instructor who taught the class.

According to an internal university memo obtained by the St. Petersburg Times, Waters apparently authorized the credit for defensive

```
September 4, 1981

MEMORANDUM

   TO:  Office of the Registrar
        34 Tigert
        Attention: Student Records

 FROM:  Wright Waters
        Instructor, EGC 3053, Summer Quarter, 1981

   RE:  Roy Elliott Harris (1 UF, SS# 261-67-1156

This memorandum is to request that Mr. Roy
Elliot Harris be added to the grade report for
EGC 3053, section 1760X, Summer Quarter, 1981.
Mr. Harris attended this class and received a
grade of ''S'' for the course. His name was not
listed on the final grade report form and there-
fore, he did not receive a final grade.
```

lineman Roy E. Harris on Sept. 4, 1981—two weeks after the class had ended and one day before the Gators opened their football schedule against the University of Miami Hurricanes.

Harris played in that game and others during the 1981 season. But it is unclear whether he actually passed the number of courses required to compete under the rules of the National Collegiate Athletic Association (NCAA).

Harris' eligibility problems apparently became known to athletic officials just a few days before the start of the season. Afraid that they might lose a key player, they reportedly approached the instructors who taught him in two other courses and appealed to get his grades raised. A better grade in either class would have made Harris eligible.

Those efforts failed, but Harris' eligibility was assured when Waters authorized the credit in his own class. That class was Student Devel-opment in a University Setting, a pass-fail course designed to help students adjust to college life.

In his memo, Waters wrote that "Harris attended this class."

The athlete, indeed, had attended and received credit for the class, but in the summer of 1980. He didn't attend a second time—in the summer of 1981—according to:

● Harris himself
● Five other football players who took the class

The graduate assistant who helped Waters teach the class says neither his records nor the course roll book show Harris attending in 1981. However, he says he thinks Waters and Harris had a special "instructor-student relationship" that may have warranted the grade. But the assistant says he knows neither the details of the relationship nor what work Harris may have performed to earn the credit. . . .

7

How to Ask Good Questions

"**M**ost reporters make a mistake by either not knowing what information they want to get from an interview or not being persistent in trying to get an answer through a combination of questions," says Sam Donaldson. "If you come with a prepared set of questions and you ask all eight of them, you clearly have missed a lot and you probably have not explored the interviewee's thoughts as you should have. You have to listen to what the person has to say, and then ask about what the person says."

The following exchange took place on "This Week With David Brinkley." The guest was Israeli Defense Minister Moshe Arens by satellite from Tel Aviv.

SAM DONALDSON: Mr. Arens, in the recent incident in the Gaza, in which terrorists captured a bus and your security forces stopped them, the story persists that one of the terrorists was led away but later killed by security forces. What are the facts?

DEFENSE MINISTER ARENS: Well, I've heard those allegations, and my guess is that they're not coming from people who are friends of Israel, and I hope that they're not coming from people who are trying to support terror.

MR. DONALDSON: You deny it then?

DEF. MIN. ARENS: Pardon?

MR. DONALDSON: You deny it, sir? It is not—

DEF. MIN. ARENS: I have no reason to give any credence to these allegations. We are at the present time running a check on the entire operation, as we always do when we have such operations, from the beginning to the end. When we will have completed the check, we will know with 100 percent certainty just exactly what happened in every one of the phases of the operation.

MR. DONALDSON: Well, you have said that terrorists who come to Israel should not expect to get away alive. What is the policy? Do you capture terrorists or do you kill them?

DEF. MIN. ARENS: We have captured many terrorists. We have also killed terrorists. When we capture a terrorist alive the next step is jail and going on trial.

Here, Donaldson stepped through several evasive responses until Arens admitted, "We have captured many terrorists. We have also killed terrorists." This is quotable. The answers that preceded this answer are not, and without Donaldson's persistent questioning, he would have nothing new, nothing interesting to report. "It all boils down to, 'What do you want to get?' " says Donaldson. "I'm looking for the news answer. The question should always have a purpose, and the purpose should be to elicit an answer that counts, that matters."

A good interviewer always tries to carry the conversation forward to new ideas, new comments. The best questions are unexpected; the best answers are spontaneous. Predictable questions elicit predictable answers and lead to a predictable story. If you are constantly recapping or reviewing old material, or you straightjacket yourself to a list of prepared questions, your interview will seem disorganized and disjointed.

You should clarify any unclear answers as you go along (see p. 73), but every question you ask should advance the interview. Questions either expand or clarify an interviewee's answers, depending on what kind of information you need.

Open-Ended and Closed-Ended Questions

To expand an interviewee's comments, you should ask *open-ended* questions. To elicit specific detail, you should ask *closed-ended* questions. In the Donaldson interview with Moshe Arens, the first question is open-ended ("What are the facts?"), and the follow-up questions alternate closed-ended ("You deny it then?") with open-ended ("What is the policy?") and then closed-ended ("Do you capture terrorists or do you kill them?"). The best interviews combine both open-ended and closed-ended questions.

An *open-ended* question (usually a "how" or a "why" question) allows the interviewee to speculate—to offer an opinion, observation or description. The interviewer who asks an open-ended question gives an opportunity for comment and direction from the interviewee. "How did you react?" or "Why do you think that happened?" are open-ended questions.

Open-ended questions elicit anecdotes. Open-ended questions invite more complete responses. An interviewee who is answering an open-ended question can choose the length and content of the answer. An open-ended question invites cooperation and participation by the interviewee. The interviewee who answers open-ended questions may also volunteer information more readily.

Open-ended questions bring anecdotes, quotations and opinion. Information from the interviewee will be more speculative and also will reflect the person's personality.

The interviewee controls the conversation more with open-ended questions than when the interviewer uses closed-ended questions.

A *closed-ended* question attempts to direct the interviewee into a specific answer: "Did you feel happy or sad?" or "How many times has this happened before?" The interviewer is indicating a choice or a desire for a numerical, quantifiable conclusion.

Closed-ended questions save time because they are more specific and usually elicit shorter answers.

Closed-ended questions are useful to obtain factual information. Precise information results from a question that is quantifiable, that will elicit a specific number or an authoritative statistic that you can use in your story.

The interviewer who needs anecdotes for a personal profile will succeed better with open-ended questions. The interview will take longer, but the interviewee will feel more trust and be more willing to volunteer anecdotes and observations. An interview with just closed-ended questions should be saved for the quick news story or for when you need several specific answers in a short time.

A combination of closed-ended and open-ended questions creates a story with both specific detail and characteristic anecdotes.

Five Interview Approaches

Before you decide which questions to ask, you should decide how to structure your interview to meet your interviewing goals. Communications researchers often isolate interviews into five different types—*funnel, inverted funnel, tunnel, covertly sequenced* and *freeform*. The best interviews combine more than one interview approach.

In a *funnel* interview, the search begins with a general idea and narrows to the important, necessary set of facts or observations. A funnel interview on a new experimental medical procedure might begin, for example, with a broad question ("Do you feel that the medical community has a responsibility to limit the scope of experimentation with animals?") and end with specific questions about a particular medical procedure ("How many genetic implants have you performed on animals in this veterinary hospital?").

Funnel interviewing is similar to courtroom questioning, where an attorney attempts to place a particular witness at a particular event, beginning with, "Have you ever visited Venice?" and ending with, "Were you at Harry's Bar and American Grill in Venice between the hours of 10:00 and 11:00 p.m. on January 5, 1991?" The approach narrows the interviewee's alternatives so that eventually the interviewee cannot avoid the specific question. Political and police reporters often use this tactic.

In an *inverted funnel* interview, the discussion begins with a narrow topic and broadens to a wider subject. A police officer questioned about brutality to prisoners might first be asked about a specific incident ("Did you see the deputy strike the suspect with the butt of his gun?"). Then, after a few more questions, the officer might be asked to speculate about law enforcement in general ("Do you feel that police officers are more or less careful about how they treat prisoners today than they were 10 years ago? Why?").

The purpose of an inverted funnel interview is to reach for an opinion, based on a foundation of gradual expansion from a specific incident or fact. Reporters who seek opinion or comment often use this approach, which gives the source credibility as an expert and then uses the source's comments to explain the story.

A *tunnel* interview strings together a series of questions about the same topic, usually all open-ended or all closed-ended (open-ended: "How did you feel when you were robbed? What did you say? How badly were you hurt?" or closed-ended: "How many robbers were there? How much money did they steal? Did they have guns?"). A tunnel interview is meant for quick observations about a specific incident and is useful for on-the-scene reactions since the questions do not invite lengthy reflection.

The interviewer in a *covertly sequenced* interview is trying to trick the interviewee by interspersing difficult with simple questions, open-ended with closed-ended questions, and friendly with antagonistic questions. In this type of interview, the interviewer mixes critical questions with unrelated questions in what seems like a random sequence.

Early in an interview, for example, you might ask a public official, "Have you ever known a public official who used campaign contributions for personal expenses?" Later you might ask, "Have you ever spent campaign contributions for personal expenses?" And then, toward the end of the interview you could ask, "How do you keep track of the way your campaign contributions are spent?" Before you used this sequence, of course, you would already have the documents that reveal the improper use of the money so that you can confront the interviewee with the information, if necessary.

By alternating different types of questions, the interviewer hopes to surprise the interviewee into an unexpected response. The interviewee often forgets what was said at the beginning of the questioning, and the interviewer uses this to juxtapose earlier responses with the answer to a later question. Covert sequencing can be especially rewarding for reporters who cover public issues.

The *freeform* interview appears to the interviewee to have little direction. A freeform interview invites open-ended responses. This is a valuable approach when you are doing a profile or when time is unlimited. The interviewer tries to test the interviewee's intellect, understand the interviewee's reasoning, and judge the intensity of the interviewee's opinions.

The interviewer in a freeform interview acts like a novelist, attempting to circumscribe the interviewee's character. You will ask many questions to provoke anecdotes, such as "Can you give me an example?" or "What do you remember about that time in your life?" Follow-up questions are essential, however, and although the interview is open-ended, it is not without direction. The alert freeform interviewer maintains the interviewee's interest and cultivates the interviewee's confidence.

Preparing the Questions

You decide the original route for the interview when you prepare your first list of questions (see Chapter 4). The list is a road but not a road map.

An interview is a journey of discovery. Sometimes you know where you are going, and sometimes you don't. You should always have an idea *why* you are interviewing someone and *what questions you want to ask*. But if the journey suddenly swerves to a side road, ride along for a while. The side road may be more interesting than the highway, and if the detour doesn't work, you can always return to the original path.

Also, don't be afraid to use other people's questions. Often interviewers ask their friends or colleagues, "If you were going to interview————, what would you want to know?" People with different interests or an outsider's viewpoint can contribute good ideas for questions.

A Listening Lesson

Every person wants an active listener, and the interviewer plays this role, as well as many others, during an interview. Listening well is your most important responsibility.

First, consider the unspoken conversation that you as an interviewer project to the interviewee. Body posture conveys distance and frigidity or closeness and intimacy. Move comfortably toward someone to indicate that you want to know more. The way you sit can say, "I'm bored" or "I'm fascinated." Don't slouch. Maintain unswerving eye contact to convince the person of your curiosity and interest. A simple gesture, such as nodding your head, can mean to an interviewee that you like what you are hearing, and the interviewee will volunteer more.

Nothing indicates better how well you have been listening than to ask an intelligent question following an interviewee's comment. But you can also use an encouraging statement, such as, "Tell me more about that. I've always been interested in that subject."As a willing student, you encourage the interviewee to become your teacher.

Often interviewees watch you take notes. When you start to write, they talk to encourage you to continue writing. But don't get so interested in your notetaking that you forget to look at the interviewee. Look up occasionally to nod encouragement or to ask another question. When you look up from your notes, an attentive interviewee will feel enough has been said and that you are ready to interject a comment or a question.

Most people also feel compelled to fill the silences in a conversation. But as an interviewer, don't ask one question quickly after another just to fill in the quiet. Often someone wants to add a comment or clarify a statement that you stifle with rat-a-tat questioning.

One central lesson that all interviewers should learn is to "shut up," according to Kristin Gilger. "Reporters talk too much. Sometimes if there is a silence, don't fill it. Silences make the reporter and the interviewee uncomfortable, but a reporter should learn to deal with the silence to see what comes from the interviewee." Let the interviewee talk.

The Best Questions

"A good question," says Sam Donaldson, "is one that's designed to spark in the person you're interviewing the desire to answer the question in an interesting and informative way. You want to have a sharp edge to the question. You don't want to say to someone, 'Well, tell me what's news.' They'll tell you, by God, and it will go on forever."

The best way to elicit an interesting, usable answer is to ask a question that cannot be misinterpreted and that asks precisely what you want the interviewee to answer. To help you ask questions, use the following guidelines to make up your list of questions before the interview. This list is only a guide, a rehearsal, for the interview. If your interviewee pursues new, interesting information, follow the interviewee's lead.

Focus on "How" and "Why" Questions

These kinds of questions ask for an opinion that will characterize the interviewee, help you evaluate the interviewee's point of view, and can lead to more sources of information than you anticipated.

Define Terms

Acronyms and technical terms are particularly vulnerable to misinterpretation. Your questions should avoid abbreviations and jargon. Also, avoid general references, such as, "At the conference you recently attended . . ." Include the name and date of the conference to ensure you are talking about the same event.

Consider the Interviewee's Viewpoint

Before you ask a question, judge your audience. By anticipating the reaction and clarifying any confusing nuances your interviewee could infer from your question, you will be sure to give the interviewee every opportunity to react to what you ask. Before you ask, for instance, "How do you feel about men who wear hairpieces?" be sure to check the head of hair you're interviewing.

Ask Questions the Interviewee Is Qualified to Answer

When you choose a qualified interviewee, the answers are guaranteed to be useful. Speculation from an unqualified observer is usually not even good background ("I didn't see the accident, but this is the way it could have happened . . ."). Quoting rumor in a story is indefensible.

Separate Yourself from Criticism of the Interviewee

To ask a difficult question, separate yourself from the interviewee's critics: "Some critics say that . . . ," or "Your opponents claim that . . ." It is even better if you have a specific criticism from a specific source to use: "District Attorney Carolyn Sanchez says that you used $3,000 of city funds to add an unnecessary security system to your garage, Mayor Hamilton. What is your reaction to the district attorney's criticism?" Quoting the opposition to the interviewee for a reaction puts you on the side of truth rather than on the side of the opposition.

Ask Questions to Which You Know the Answers

If you are dealing with an evasive source, target some of the questions to verify the interviewee's position. "I did a story on how the St. Petersburg Yacht Club accepts its members, all of whom happen to be white," says Sandra Thompson.

"I had to ask questions like, 'Do you have any black members?' I knew they didn't, but I needed to have the interviewee say they didn't. 'How do you select your members?' They'd laugh and answer in generalities, 'The same as any other private club.' So then I had to ask, 'Well, what do other private clubs do?' They sound like stupid questions, but they're obvious questions that have to be asked, not for the sake of the question, but for the source of the answer so you can quote the person."

If You Don't Ask, You Won't Get an Answer

Because they are afraid to appear ignorant, many reporters hesitate to ask simple questions, then learn that simple questions often lead to interesting, quotable answers. Remember that Ted Koppel says an interviewer must be willing to become "the deliberate witless."

As an interviewer, he assumes "that there are always going to be a couple of million people who have never heard of baseball, or who don't know anything about economics, or who couldn't care less about foreign policy, or who really have not struggled with the issue of politics and religion. For each of these people, this has nothing to do with their general level of intelligence. The subject is just not something that happens to fascinate them." It is better to ask too many questions than too few.

Follow-Up Questions That Clarify

When you ask a question, in a split-second conscious or subconscious reaction, your interviewee decides (1) whether to answer the question and (2) how to answer the question. With the same speed, you must decide whether the answer you receive is complete. If so, continue to another topic. If not, pursue your point with one or more follow-up questions.

For example, an aerospace corporation president tells you she does not know the origin of toxic chemicals that have leaked into the river near the aerospace plant. Some good follow-up questions might be, "Do you use toxic chemicals in the manufacture of rocket fuels?" Then you could ask, "Are those toxic chemicals released into the river?" and then, "When and in what quantities were those chemicals released?" and then, "Do your own chemists monitor the river's toxicity level?" and finally, "What do the chemists' reports show?" The president still can claim she doesn't remember, but at least you have explored several possible explanations. If she evades the questions, you can quote her forgetfulness.

Some other good follow-ups to clarify an answer are questions that:

Set Limits to Define the Answer

If your interviewee gives you a general answer, use prescriptive limits to define the answer (greater than . . . less than; before June . . . after June; larger than . . . smaller than). Bonnie Kettner says she used this technique when she was reporting on the Insurance Corporation of British Columbia (ICBC), which oversees all the insurance coverage for British Columbia.

"I phoned them up, and the man said, 'I can't give you that information.' But I could tell from his voice that he was willing to play ball, so I said, 'Well, from what I understand—and I took a guess—the rates are going up 30 percent.' And he said, 'Oh, I think your sources are a bit high on that.' Then I said, 'Well, there's another source who told me it was 15 percent.' So he said, 'That's a bit low.' So I said, 'If I talk about 20 percent in the newspaper, I guess I won't be too far off.' And he said, 'You can print what you want.' "

Ask for Rankings

This technique helps your interviewee evaluate choices. You can, for example, ask for a best-to-worst ranking, a numbered ranking (1 to 10), or a most-to-least choice. Your story, however, should report that the interviewee was asked to rank alternatives.

Give an Either/Or Choice

Another closed-ended technique that is less reliable, but sometimes effective, is to ask your interviewee to choose between two alternatives, as Sam Donaldson did with Moshe Arens ("Do you capture terrorists or do you kill them?"). Again, you should report in the story that the interviewee's choices were limited.

Restate the Answer

If you aren't sure exactly what the interviewee is saying, clarify by reviewing the answer ("Are you saying that . . .?"). Your interviewee will appreciate your effort to completely understand the answer. If you have misunderstood, it's better to find out during the interview rather than after your story appears.

Clarify Generalizations

An interviewee might say, "We've had two robberies in our neighborhood in the last six months. This is a crime wave." Ask what other evidence the interviewee has for the statement. The interviewee may have statistics but more likely is generalizing from personal experience rather than from verifiable data.

Translate Jargon

If your interviewee uses an acronym (for example, ARM, which stands for adjustable rate mortgage) or an unfamiliar term, wait until a logical break in the conversation. Then ask for a definition. "That's a new term to me. Could you define it?" is a polite way of saying, "You're talking over my head."

Verify Statistics and Dates

Except for the most obvious statistics, such as their birth date or their own age, interviewees often are casual about dates and numbers. As the interview proceeds, double-check statistics and dates with the interviewee. Then, at the conclusion of the interview, ask where you can find a verifiable record of the information you need.

Determine Sequence

The order in which events happen is often as important as the events themselves. "Did you get married before or after you became a Marine?"

"Was Stella your third or fourth wife?" Remember to review the sequence of events.

Ask for Specific Sources

When an interviewee cannot answer your question, ask, "Who would you ask if you wanted to know the answer?" Make sure you ask for specific names and phone numbers rather than accepting a general reference to the name of a department, company or public agency where you might find the information.

Follow-Up Questions That Expand

Some interviewees give you a one-word answer and nothing more. The "Yes," "No," "Maybe" interviewee is every interviewer's nightmare. "Avoiding questions by just giving monosyllabic answers is terribly effective," says Ted Koppel. "The fact is that the interviewee can say more 'Yeps' and 'Nopes' than you can come up with questions. Plus, the less the interviewee says, the less chance there is that he or she will trip up."

Here are some follow-ups to take you beyond "Yes," "No" and "Maybe."

Enlarge on a Specific Incident

A description of a specific event often becomes a metaphor for a person's entire personality. A single example from something you've learned about someone can provoke a worthwhile response. "I read that every year you retreat to the mountains for a month and camp out away from newspapers, newspeople and the telephone. What do you think you gain from this experience?"

Remember Your Sense of History

If you juxtapose someone's past opinions or actions with that person's present behavior, you usually can encourage an interesting comment. "Governor, you visited the Senior Citizens Housing Project last week and announced that this is a good example of business and government working together to build a useful program for the elderly. Yet last year your administration opposed the program that built this project. What is the administration's current position on privately financed housing for the elderly?"

Ask "Why Do You Say That?"

Sam Donaldson says that one of the simplest questions is "Why do you say that?" According to Donaldson, "It's also a dodge if you haven't heard the answer. But I'm always living for the day when I'll ask, 'Why do you say that?' and the guy answers, 'Because I want to.'"

Ask for an Example

When a private detective says, "I learned early that it's easy to find out very personal information about people just by asking their neighbors," you say, "Can you give an example?" or "Can you describe a time when that happened to you?" The answer to the follow-up will be much more interesting than the detective's general statement.

Ask for a Chronology

"And then what happened after that?" "And what happened after that?" If you take an event apart, your interviewee will remember more detail than if you say, "Tell me what happened." Someone might say, "Then the tornado struck." If you stop there, you have no usable details.

Reflect the Person's Feelings

If someone's home was deliberately destroyed by an arsonist yesterday, today the person may say, "I feel fine now." You can recapture yesterday's emotion if you say, "I'll bet you were scared." Mentioning the emotion forces the person to relive not only yesterday's experience but also yesterday's feelings and thoughts.

Play Personal Counselor

Some interviewers use the "You show me yours, and I'll show you mine" approach. Sharing an intimacy often elicits a similar intimacy from the interviewee. This can become a counseling session, however, so use this tactic sparingly.

Display Your Ignorance

Another approach to be used selectively is "Poor Me." Appear to understand less than you do. Humbly note your ignorance by saying, for instance, "I'm not an attorney, but it seems to me that . . ." To raise you out of your ignorant dilemma, the interviewee explains with simpler language and new information.

Surprise Your Interviewee with an Emotional Reaction

An unusual approach that sometimes works is to make a statement such as, "Well, that's outrageous! How can they get away with that?" Your interviewee, poised for a question instead of a statement, may react spontaneously to your outrage and enlarge on it.

Make a Deliberately Inaccurate Statement

If someone is being evasive, challenge the person with a deliberate error. "I've heard you and your partner made only $5 million profit on that apartment house sale" (when you have heard figures ranging from $10 million to $100 million). People cannot resist correcting an inaccuracy, especially about themselves.

Be Aware of What Hasn't Been Said

A clever interviewee can avoid answering the questions you ask (see p. 105). As you proceed through an interview, detach yourself from the conversation for just a few moments every once in a while to analyze what has been left out. Then ask about the omission—"I've noticed that you haven't mentioned . . ."

Repeat the Question

Someone can unintentionally or deliberately answer a question you did not ask. An interviewee who has prepared before the interview to give you certain information will try to insert that information in the conversation whether it fits or not. If the information conflicts with or bypasses what you want to know, say, "But that wasn't my question" or "Let me repeat my question; I'm not sure I've explained what I want to know." If someone is being truly evasive, say, "You're not answering my question. My question is . . ."

Maintain Your Critical Sense

While you interview someone, analyze the person's possible motives in answering or evading your questions. Sometimes a comment like "You're not telling me this just because I'm a reporter, are you?" causes the person to justify the answer.

Use Five Seconds of Silence

A five-second pause after a difficult question offers your interviewee time to consider, to clarify and often to volunteer more information than you expect. When a conversation moves nonstop, the interviewee has very little opportunity to reconsider or to expand on an answer. A pause, coupled with an interested, curious look from the interviewer, offers surprising rewards. In this same category, some interviewers say they can elicit unexpected answers from a practiced interviewee by feigning indifference.

Interviewees Who Talk but Do Not Answer

A clever interviewee will not refuse to answer your questions but instead will offer interminable verbal nothings. "I'm not really lied to very often," says Sam Donaldson. "I'm turned aside and disregarded, and I'm not given an answer frequently—in fact, at the White House most of the time. But the smart ones never lie. Occasionally, you run across someone dumb, but they don't do it more than once."

You must be able to detect quickly the interviewee who appears to be talking but instead is producing verbal air. Interviewees will avoid answering a difficult question by:

Using the Elephant and the Ant Technique

With this technique, usually called *bridging*, the interviewee transfers the conversation from an unfamiliar or uncomfortable subject to one more familiar or more comfortable. Ted Koppel calls this the "elephant and the ant" technique.

"Every college student at one time or another has had the experience of being given a question they really have not studied," says Koppel. "The question is on elephants, and they say, 'Elephants are extraordinarily large creatures, in marked contrast to the ant,' which they *have* studied. The student then proceeds to give a long dissertation about the ant.

"So the elephant-ant technique is very useful, where the interviewee begins by saying, 'I'm very glad you asked me about my voting record, Mr. Koppel, because in point of fact I have been in office, as you know, for 20 years and I recall 20 years ago when I came here . . . ,' and before you know it, they're off on another subject."

Answering a Question You Did Not Ask

This is a variety of bridging. The interviewee listens to your question and then gives you an answer that is totally unrelated. "I have often wondered about that myself," says the interviewee, "but that is not the real issue here. The real issue is . . . "

Asking You a Question

The interviewee answers a question with a question. The interviewer then becomes the interviewee and loses control. The interviewer asks, "In Miami last night, 15 people were arrested for organizing an alleged marijuana smuggling ring. As chief attorney for the Americans for Sane Marijuana Laws, what role will you play in their defense?" The interviewee answers, "We haven't been contacted yet by any of the people who were arrested. How many suspects have the police positively identified?"

Denying the Obvious

If the question is "Your budget cuts have hurt the poor. Why?" The interviewee can simply say, "My budget cuts have not hurt the poor. We are spending more this year than at any time in our history," which may be correct but only because of inflation. The real dollar amount is considerably less this year than five years ago because today's dollar buys less.

Giving a Vague Response

"You'll ask someone, 'Did you take the money?' " says Bill Nottingham. "He'll say, 'Are you serious? I've never done a dishonest thing in my life.' Well, maybe he took the money and didn't think it was dishonest."

Faking It

"The assumption has to be on the part of the person being interviewed that nine times out of 10, he knows more about his subject than you do," says Ted Koppel. "So he can give you a response that is not entirely accurate, and by the time you find out that it's not entirely accurate, the interview's over."

Telling a Joke or an Anecdote

A good joke will divert an interviewer's attention from just about any subject. "You've asked a good question. That reminds me of the joke about . . ." The longer the joke lasts, the longer the interviewer must remember the original question.

Asking You to Check Back Later

This interviewee makes a dutiful notation of your question and tells you he or she doesn't know the answer but will find the answer and call you back later. This person hopes you will forget to ask again or to telephone later. Often you do forget, or the answer comes too late to report.

Questioning Your Motives, Manners or Competence

More than one interviewer has been intimidated by a clever interviewee who quipped, "Now, why would you say a horrible thing like that about a nice person like me?" or "A rude question like that doesn't deserve a response!" or "That's the stupidest question I ever heard!" or "That's not important."

"The first time someone says, 'You're a lousy reporter,' or 'You're a stupid stinker to ask a question like that,' you shrink back like a flower," says Bonnie Kettner. "The next time it happens, it doesn't mean anything. You simply carry on because you know what you've got to do."

Rejecting the Question as Too Intrusive

In a press conference or a group interview, if a reporter's question might possibly be viewed by other reporters as tasteless or impertinent, the person can turn other reporters against the questioner. The interviewee simply implies that the reporter has intruded on personal privacy, and the embarrassed reporter may drop the idea to save face among colleagues. "I don't think whether I've had an abortion or not is any of your business, Mr.————, and I think your colleagues have better sense than to ask such a personal question."

Using "No Comment"

Rarely will an experienced interviewee use this dodge. Inexperienced interviewees who have seen television portrayals of evasive interviewees think that "no comment" will work. The best follow-up question to a "no comment" answer is, "Why don't you want to comment?" Then you can use the explanation to ask more questions.

You interview an author and ask, "Do you expect to make a lot of money from this book?" The author says, "I don't really want to comment on that." You say, "Why don't you want to tell me how much you hope to make? We all have to make a living, don't we?" The author says, "Yes." You say, "Well, how good a living do you expect to make from this book?" and follow through from there.

Remember that any evasive answer can be counteracted by a good follow-up question. A good interviewer wants a response that is accurate and characteristic of the interviewee. Keep asking questions until you have given your interviewee every chance to answer completely.

The Worst Questions

Just as good initial and follow-up questions ensure usable answers, poor questions ensure unquotable material. Do not ask:

Two-Part Questions

An interviewee trying to concentrate on the sequence of your questions will be confused if you ask two questions simultaneously. Ask one question at a time.

Questions Including Simultaneous Opposites

An interviewee who is asked to comment on the advantages and dis-advantages or the right and the wrong way or the best and the worst, for example, will answer the first part of the question and not the second. Ask for the advantages (or the right way or the best) first; then ask for the disadvantages (or the wrong way or the worst).

"Whether-or-Not" Questions

This is related to simultaneous opposites, and the response can be just as misleading. You ask, "Can you tell me whether or not you plan to run for office?" The interviewee says, "No." Does this mean that the inter-viewee plans not to run for office, or that the interviewee doesn't want to tell you whether he will run for office? You may infer the wrong infor-mation. Ask, instead, "Will you run for office?" which elicits a specific response.

Questions Longer Than Two Sentences

A question longer than two sentences is a speech, not a question. Your interviewee will lose interest by the third sentence, and by that time, you will forget your first sentence. The limit on questions is two sentences.

Unfocused Questions and Nonquestions

A question that asks for nothing from the interviewee gets nothing. "That was a wonderful game you had there, sport!" or "Has anything happened within the last 24 hours that you want to comment on?" or "Tell me a funny story."

Questions That Begin with an Apology

If you anticipate an interviewee's response, you point out a reason not to answer your question even before you ask the question: "I know this may seem to be an embarrassing (trivial, stupid, tasteless) question, but . . ." The interviewee may quickly decide that the question is embarrassing (trivial, stupid, tasteless) and refuse to answer.

Cliché Questions

Questions that have been asked repeatedly will get answers that have been given repeatedly. "How did you feel when you won the lottery?" ("Wonderful.") "Is it hot (cold) enough for you?" ("Yes" or "No.") "What have you been doing?" ("Not much.")

Leading Questions

An interviewer should try to maintain neutrality. A leading question ("When did you stop killing yourself with alcohol?") assumes a point of view and betrays the interviewer's perspective. First, the interviewee must deny the alcoholism and then deal with the implied comment that the interviewee is self-destructive. This approach invites belligerence.

"Yes-or-No" Questions

Questions that invite comment usually are more useful than questions that can be answered with "Yes" or "No." If you have a chance for a follow-up, such as "Explain that for me," a "Yes" or "No" answer can be very useful. If you don't have a chance for a follow-up, such as at a press conference or in a rushed, on-the-spot interview, you are left with only a "Yes" or "No" quote that is rarely usable.

Absolute Questions

Few people respond well to a statement containing absolutes. Questions that use contentious verbs (such as *forbid* or *destroy*), or questions that include limiting adverbs (such as *completely, certainly* or *positively*), usually produce equivocation and animosity rather than a quotable answer.

On- and Off-the-Record Information

Reporters use the following terms to describe the agreements they make with interviewees about how they will use information from an interview:

1. *On the record.* The reporter can publish everything that is discussed.

2. *Not for attribution.* The reporter can use the information without naming the specific person who gave the information.

3. *On background.* The reporter can use the information, using a general title as the source ("a State Department official said").

4. *Off the record.* The reporter will use the information only for personal background and perspective and will not publish the information or the source of information.

These categories seem clear. But someone who says "This is off the record" often means "This is not for attribution. I'll tell you, but just don't hang my name on the information." (See Chapter 11 for more information about the potential legal consequences of quoting anonymous sources.)

Kristin Gilger says, "I will say to an interviewee, 'I am not going to write this down, but explain it to me because I am having trouble understanding this.' Later in the interview, I will back up and try to get the comment on the record. I rephrase questions I asked at the first part of the interview that the interviewee was reluctant to talk about at first."

A reporter dealing with off-the-record conversations should always clarify any limits the interviewee wants to put on the information in an interview. "What you don't want to do is leave the interview with a misunderstanding between you and your source," says Bill Nottingham. "If people go to the trouble to give you the information, and you agree to protect them, that's the deal. You protect them or you don't call yourself a journalist."

A Final Word

These interviewing suggestions will help you only if your curiosity compels you to find an answer to every question you ask. Persistence is just as important as how you phrase the question. Even if you stumble at first over some of your questions, the interviewer who is interested, curious and persistent always gets a good story.

■■■■■   AN   INTERVIEWING   CASE   STUDY

Maryln Schwartz
The Dallas Morning News

Maryln Schwartz graduated from the University of Georgia and has been a reporter at *The Dallas Morning News* since 1971. She has worked as a general assignment reporter and as a special writer and is now a columnist. She has won 16 awards for feature writing from the Texas Associated Press and from United Press International, as well as four Penney-Missouri Awards from the University of Missouri.

In this example, Schwartz shows how an idea often takes several interviews before it becomes a story.

"Since I write a column, everything I run into I think of as a column. Coming up with three new ideas a week is hard. I'm always looking for ideas.

"I kept running across recipes that said 'Better Than Sex Cake' or 'Better Than Sex Cookies,' and then I saw the cover [of *Ladies Home Journal*] about 'Better Than Sex Recipes.' I also had been noticing that for a long time there had been all the talk about safe sex. I had just been to a meeting that was very serious, talking to the community about precautions. And when I saw that cover of the *Ladies Home Journal*, I just started laughing.

"A lot of recipes were around that said they were better than sex— cakes, cookies and a lot of dessert dishes. And I kind of said it as a joke to somebody: 'Oh yeah? Who's tested that? How far does this go?'

"I had the recipes. I had taken some from the *Ladies Home Journal*, and I had the recipes I'd gotten in a cookbook for Christmas. I gave some recipes out to a few people to try and then tell me what they thought.

"It takes a lot to get people to take the time to do those things. Some people think it's a lot of fun, and some people don't. I had about six or seven test people. I interviewed them on the phone and talked to them in person. And I made some of the recipes myself. Then I called the food editor of the *Ladies Home Journal*, and she had a good sense of humor about it.

"I worked on this story over a two-week period. I usually have a couple of things going at once. It was not a hard column to write once I got all the stuff together, but it took two weeks to do the research.

"Sometimes ideas seem good when you talk about them, but it's just a quick idea, like a quick joke, and you can't make a whole column out of it. So I had to make sure that I had enough information to make a whole column.

"Everybody looks at somebody else's job and thinks it's so easy. People are always asking me what I do after I do those little columns. And I say, 'I go to medical school. If the column falls through, I can always fall back on brain surgery.' They really think that all it takes is an hour. And it doesn't.

"Also, whenever you deal with a subject like that, you need to be *very* careful. You worry about bad taste because you never know what's going to turn the reader off. When I turned it [the column] in, I said [to my editor], 'I don't think this is in bad taste, but what do you think?' She said, 'No. This is fine.'

"I don't mind if I stir things up. I don't mind being controversial. I want people to talk about me, and I don't mind if they get mad at me. I just want to make sure I'm correct and that I haven't taken a cheap shot because it's really easy to take cheap shots in writing a column. I don't care how mad people get if I know that I've been fair.

"I got a lot of good response to the column. People enjoyed it. I was surprised that I didn't get any negative response because, usually when you talk about sex, there's always someone out there to criticize. But there was no negative response at all. It was fun."

Can Food Be Better Than Sex?

By Maryln Schwartz
The Dallas Morning News

This is not an x-rated column. But in the interest of good reporting, I must point out that a lot of people these days are carrying the "safe sex" campaign one step further.

For Christmas, I received a cookbook that offers four recipes for "better than sex cake." A few weeks later, I was at a restaurant in New Orleans that featured "better than sex icebox chocolate pie." Then last month, I found that even the usually traditional Ladies Home Journal offered a bonus food section.

You guessed it. "Better than sex desserts."

Where did these names come from? And even more important, was there a test kitchen?

First I copied the recipes in the Journal and passed them around to a few cooks who are willing to try new things. I explained that the magazine called these dishes a "cache of truly wicked treats." I wanted them to make the desserts in the privacy of their own kitchens.

I assured them that this was strictly scientific. Their names would never be mentioned. They didn't even have to sign their reports. But I wanted honest answers.

Were the Chocolate Macadamia Nut Terrine and the frozen tiramisu really "better than sex"? And what about the tequila-spiked fresh fruit with vanilla ice cream? Just how sinful is it?

The test cooks were to send me their findings in a plain Manila envelope.

Researcher "A" called the Chocolate Macadamia Nut Terrine "pretty fantastic." But her findings were inconclusive.

"I find there are shadings to this test," she wrote. "It all depends. Do you want to know if this [dessert] is better than sex *with whom*?"

Researcher "B" said he was not usually a fancy cook, so he spent hours putting together the frozen tiramisu (a dessert featuring brandy, espresso, mascarpone cheese, chocolate ice cream and chocolate-coated coffee beans, finely chopped in a food processor). It took him an hour just to brew the espresso, whip the cream and hunt up some coffee-flavored liqueur.

"I'm not sure if this is better than sex," he said. "But I can tell you this. Sex is a lot easier."

In my own research, I found that "better than sex cake" has been around for some time. But in the past, there have been only two basic recipes. One for a chocolate cake and one for a yellow cake. Now there are six or seven recipes calling for everything from pineapple and a cup of sour cream to chocolate fudge, chocolate chips and chocolate shavings.

I had planned to call a psychologist and ask if she thought all these new "better than sex" recipes were pointing toward a viable "safe sex" substitute.

Then I decided it wasn't a valid question. Those cakes call for an abundance of butter, sour cream, eggs, milk and chocolate. They can't be called safe. The cholesterol alone could kill you.

Jan Harard, the food editor of Ladies Home Journal, says readers' response to the recipes has been negative.

"Some readers said they did not feel that it was tasteful to equate sex with food."

She says the magazine ran a "better than sex cake" recipe a few years ago and got positive feedback.

"I think it's a sign of the times," she says. "People are becoming more puritanical."

There was still one test left. I myself made up a "better than sex cake" (the one that calls for chocolate butter cake mix, chocolate pudding, chocolate chips and sour cream) and served it to six guests.

"OK," I said. "This is a test. Was that cake really better than sex?"

Everyone was understandably a bit shy about discussing such a delicate subject.

But after finishing the cake, two of the men lit up cigarettes.

8

How to Interview for Broadcast

If time is an ogre for print reporters, then for broadcast journalists, time is truly a tyrant. A broadcast reporter has less time to prepare and research than a print reporter, and broadcast interviews are typically shorter than print. Often broadcast reporters must tell a story in 30 to 60 seconds. In the fast-paced world of broadcasting, a two-minute story seems like a minidocumentary. The 11-second epithet, the 14-second one-liner make news because they are packaged as tightly as the newscast itself.

Public officials know this. They massage public presentations to offer up tidy, bundled quotes. They polish their interview responses to get air time in the competitive whirl of the day's news. Broadcast reporters often understand the game, almost welcome it, because a good, tight quote makes a good, tight story. Why ask for more?

Because there is more. Like all good reporters, a good broadcast reporter doesn't want what everyone else has. A good broadcast reporter must be able to interview not only people prepared to be interviewed but also people who have never been near a microphone. A good broadcast reporter wants to have something worthwhile to put on the air. A good broadcast reporter wants the interview to be interesting to watch.

"I have some sort of a reputation for asking flamboyant or aggressive questions, but I have never, ever attempted to do that," says Sam Donaldson. "I have sometimes asked aggressive questions and needled guests and all of that, but it's because I want information, not because I want a show.

"Now, I'm no dummy. If I can get that information and it's interesting and it's interestingly presented, I think that's fine. I think, to get an audience, you have to not be dull.

"Howard K. Smith told me in the early '60s that the worst sin in television news is to be dull. I thought that was silly. I thought the worst sin must be to be inaccurate, or biased, or incomplete.

"But, I am convinced Howard is right. Because if you are dull, no matter how responsible, or how accurate, or how unbiased, or how complete the rest of what you say is—if no one is listening, it doesn't matter. It simply doesn't matter."

How Broadcast Interviews Differ from Print

Broadcast reporters are part of the interview in a way print reporters are not. Often the audience hears the questions a broadcast reporter asks, whereas a newspaper reader rarely knows the questions that produce the story. Television reporters also are often seen in an interview—whether it's full-face or as part of a shoulder leaning into a shot of the interviewee.

The interviewee's role in a broadcast interview differs, too. Some people yearn to be on the air, but often an interviewee who talks easily to a print reporter with a notebook hesitates to be interviewed for broadcast. An interviewee may be self-conscious about a stutter or worry that he needs a haircut. Except in the rare interview where someone's voice or face is disguised or the interviewee hides behind a screen, a broadcast interview is on the record for everyone to hear and see. You can't have a voice or a face on the air without a name. It's pretty difficult to introduce someone by saying, "Here's No-Name."

A broadcast interview puts other barriers between the reporter and the interviewee, from a tape recorder and a microphone to what one reporter called "the thousand pound pencil"—cameras, lights, sound equipment and the people who go with them. A broadcast reporter's product relies on equipment. When a tape erases itself, or a camera runs out of tape, you lose the story.

Television also shows more than it tells. The audience hears or sees unfiltered reactions from the interviewee, so description of the interviewee or the interviewee's reaction is unnecessary. The first shock of a tragedy or the first response to a pointed question is instantly available. Broadcast portrays more immediate personal emotion—the living quote.

Broadcast offers immediacy and access. Print gives reflection and review. Broadcast compresses, print expands. Broadcast offers information rather than explanation. A newspaper reader can review a print story several times. Broadcast gives the listener/viewer less time to think and to absorb because the stories move quickly, and (on television) so do the pictures.

Broadcast interviewers share many characteristics with print interviewers, but broadcast interviewers are limited more by time and equipment. Broadcast interviewers can use sounds and pictures as shorthand to enhance a story, but print reporters have only words to convey sights and sounds. Each type of interview offers a separate challenge.

How to Prepare for a Broadcast Interview

Although broadcast interviewers use basically the same approach as print interviewers, the circumstance and the time restraints make it essential for broadcast interviewers to focus the topic, to be conscious of the equipment, and to define the goal of each interview before the interview begins.

Remember the Focus

No matter how little time you have, you should think about the interview's central theme. What one topic will you discuss? What one issue will you explore? "I think it's good to go in with a sense of what it is you want to happen in the course of the conversation," says Susan Stamberg. "What points do you want to get made? What information do you want to elicit? Then you have to be ready to abandon that at any moment if something comes up that you hadn't thought about before, but that strikes you as far more interesting."

Stamberg says she recommends practicing the interview beforehand. Say to yourself, "First I'll ask this, and the response will be this. Then I'll ask this, and this is what the person will say." You won't be entirely accurate, of course, but you will be more prepared than if you did not anticipate the conversation at all.

Try to develop a sequence of questions to order the interviewee's thoughts and your own as you go, but don't tie yourself to a list. "The biggest mistake is coming in with a list of 10 questions and then not paying any attention to the answers that are being given," says Stamberg. "The guest may get off on a tangent, but it can be much more interesting than anything you've got on paper." The questions should logically progress from one another, grow out of comments in the interview, anticipate what your audience wants to know.

During an interview, when your follow-up questions coincide with what your listener wants to know, your interview is successful. Organization and forethought are important to a broadcast interviewer because you have less time than a print interviewer. Your questions can't wander. Your ignorance shows too easily.

Remember the Equipment

A broadcast reporter can't work alone. You must adjust to your equipment. Radio reporters usually need just a tape recorder and a microphone. Television sometimes needs not only a camera and sound equipment but lights and the people who make all the equipment work. A television reporter is a manager—of equipment and people—as well as a reporter.

Once you've mastered the equipment and the people who go along with it, however, you must understand how strange this setup seems to some interviewees. In the field, a cadre of broadcast people at a news event changes the character of the event. Even one television camera can transform a seemingly shy public official into a camera hog or scare away a private person who has just given four interviews to print reporters.

In the studio, television adds makeup, a set, hot lights and a teleprompter. Radio adds an oversize microphone, a crowded table and rows of dials that seem complicated enough to make you part of the U.S. space program.

Whether you interview for radio or television, on the telephone, in the field, or in the studio, be sensitive to an interviewee's possible fears and hesitations. Don't assume that anyone, except the most prominent public figure, understands the process as well as you do. If you explain how the equipment works and how long the two of you will talk, you reassure the interviewee and show that you care.

Whenever possible, don't rush the interviewee or yourself. Think of this extra time as the time you would use in a print interview to establish rapport. The interviewee needs time to become comfortable with you, to hear your voice, to look at your face, and to understand the situation before you both can talk easily.

Remember Your Goal

Like a print interview, a broadcast interview is an artificial conversation, but your goal should always be to capture your interviewee's attention so well that the person forgets the equipment and the audience and talks to just you.

"The most illuminating ideas come out of the interplay between the person being interviewed and the reporter," says ABC's John Martin. "Here are two minds at work, two people talking to each other, and the audience gets to sit in on that. There are certain moments when somebody in the audience connects with somebody on camera. Almost through the heart, through the gut, viewers have a chance to get an insight they didn't have before."

Interviews on the Phone and in the Field

Your interviews can be live or on tape, on the telephone, in the field, or in the studio. You can be covering a breaking news event or preparing a news feature. All broadcast interviews share the need for succinct questions and answers, good pacing and interest. But the circumstances of the interview dictate what an interviewer should remember.

Telephone Interviews

Television usually uses a telephone interview only when the event happens so close to air time that pictures are unavailable, or when someone conducts a call-in show from a studio. A telephone interview is a staple for many radio reporters, who call up experts and eyewitnesses for quick advice or a timely comment. Telephone interviews, either live or on tape, also give an interviewer access to a world of experts and issues outside the local community.

A taped interview offers you more freedom because you can talk longer and then edit for the best sound bites after the interview. You can interview several people and use the most articulate speaker. You can even throw out a bad interview and start over.

A live telephone interview, like all live interviews, makes you an on-the-spot editor. You must pace and clarify the questions and the answers as you go.

The telephone is a quick way to interview. (For more tips about telephone interviews in general, see pp. 71–75.) People usually consent easily to an interview on the phone. The telephone is familiar, unintimidating. People don't have to interrupt their schedules, they don't have to worry about an audience, and they don't have to dress up.

Telephone interviews can, however, hinder an interviewer. You have only someone's words without a face. If you are interviewing someone you don't know, you must create intimacy quickly for a conversation that may last for less than 15 minutes. Remember to:

1. *Develop familiarity.* For a discussion about a personal topic, ask permission to call the person by his or her first name. Encourage the

interviewee to call you by your first name. For an official conversation, always use the appropriate Mr., Mrs., Miss or Ms. Check the interviewee's preference before the interview begins.

2. *Smile through the telephone.* You must seem interested, receptive. To do this on the telephone, you must almost overplay your role of fascination with the subject. Don't condescend to your interviewee, but remember that the interviewee can't look in your eyes and see your excitement. Your voice must be upbeat.

3. *Explain the process.* Federal Communications Commission rules require that you tell the interviewee that everything that is said may be used on the air. Also, if you are taping the interview, you can assure the person that there will be a second chance, if necessary. If you are live, explain that you will need short answers and that you may have to interrupt occasionally.

4. *Reassure the interviewee.* When someone says, "Oh, I'm so nervous," tell the person that you're often nervous, too (which is usually more accurate than the interviewee could ever understand). Empathize with the interviewee's anxiety.

5. *Explain the order of the interview beforehand.* Explain what the main focus of your questions will be, without listing the specific questions, so that the person will be somewhat prepared.

6. *Carefully track the conversation,* once you begin the interview. It is easy for a telephone interviewee to become distracted and to ramble because there are no signals other than your voice. Follow the dialogue carefully, and interrupt gently when the answer gets too long or off the point.

7. *Watch the "uh-huhs."* Any "uh-huh" you say in a taped interview will have to be edited out of the sound bite to make the piece usable. In a live interview, the "uh-huhs" distract the listener/viewer.

8. *Vary the sequence of questions.* One question-answer after another is not as interesting to your listeners/viewers as a question-answer followed by your asking the interviewee what he means. Then the listener catches two people in the act of thinking.

9. *Listen.* Especially in a telephone conversation, you can easily ask a question that has no relationship to the comment the person just made because you are preoccupied. Take notes to help maintain your interest.

Field Interviews

The majority of broadcast reporters spend their time running around the countryside chasing breaking news and news feature stories—to be used either live or on tape. Half this job is jumping in and out of cars and vans, working your way through a crowd, missing stoplights, and rushing to get on the air.

What kinds of interviewees should you look for? John Martin says he divides interviewees in the field into three categories. First, find the established people in the field, whose expertise is recognized. "This carries with it all the negative stereotypes of the Establishment," says Martin. "But the Establishment only gets established because it does things somehow effectively or in some manner that gets recognized as competent or credible. Ralph Nader is as much the Establishment as the head of the Federal Aviation Administration. He has established himself as a critic whose research is good."

Second, look for people at the lower level who really make the system work—whether an air traffic controller or a presidential campaign adviser. "You look for people in the system who are not in positions of authority, but who understand or live in the circumstance you are trying to portray," Martin says.

The third category is "what I would call the Wild Card," he says. "I'm always looking for a person who is not part of the system, who is not an authority, but who is passing through, an outside observer whose view is a little more informed than mine because this is the first day I've looked at the subject. I call it a Wild Card because I never know, going into a situation, whether I'm going to find one."

Another important part of the job is convincing someone to speak with you on the air. Getting the interview sometimes is more work than doing the interview.

As a broadcast interviewer, you can use the same approach as a print reporter who wants someone to talk (see p. 59). When possible, phone ahead to organize the time and place you will talk. If someone says no on the spot, ask at least one more time and then find someone else. If you need the interview, wait. Find out where the person will be and catch the interviewee when he or she doesn't expect you. Be persistent, but don't be pushy.

Matt Levi says he used to think he had a right to interview anyone, anytime. "I used to burst in, thinking this was television. By the nature of the medium, though, I realized we can ruin somebody's career on a Saturday, and it won't even make the news on Monday."

Levi says that, whenever possible, he liked to take the time to visit his subjects beforehand without a camera. When he wanted someone to talk about a sensitive subject on camera, he explained that no one can portray the emotion as vividly as someone who has had the experience.

"I contacted 100 people for my series on pregnant women who used drugs and alcohol. Two of the ladies' babies had died. One woman had an abortion. One of the ladies was shooting up heroin in the delivery room. I got six women to talk, but I don't feel I have a right to badger someone into appearing. If I feel myself being argumentative, I just drop it."

Not every interviewee makes good television. The person you choose to interview is a significant part of the success of your interview. Sometimes the interviewee is prearranged—a celebrity, a public official or someone prepared to talk about a breaking news or feature news topic. For any on-camera field interview, remember:

1. *Talk with the person for a while to test what they know.* Look for someone who is articulate, outspoken and willing. Beware of an exuberant volunteer who waves both arms in the air when you are looking for someone to be interviewed on camera.

2. *Focus the topic and prepare the interviewee quickly.* Remember to explain how the equipment works if the person seems uncomfortable.

3. *Talk the interview through in a general way.* Try not to ask the person too many questions beforehand because the on-the-air interview will be practiced and the person may say, "Well, as I told you before . . ."

4. *Phrase your questions carefully so that you will be able to use one cut with the question and answer.* This is to avoid a voice-over introduction to the answer when you write the script, or a cutaway where you are not in the shot with the interviewee—you ask the question in one shot, and then the interviewee answers in a separate shot. The audience gets more of a feel for the mind working on both sides, but especially on the side of the interviewee, when the audience hears the question and then the person's reaction.

5. *Anticipate the answer to your question.* "One of the techniques that works with most people," says Sam Donaldson, "is that if you ask the question in a way that you give them a quote, often they'll give it back to you. Now, this isn't a trick in any underhanded way. This crystallizes the response and gives them a springboard."

If you say to a gubernatorial candidate, for example, "The in-cumbent governor says you aren't telling the truth on taxes," the candidate may answer, "The governor isn't telling the truth on taxes. I have said . . ." Remember that when you want a news answer, you are looking for a succinct response that you can use verbatim.

6. *If you must ask your interviewee to repeat an answer, try to ask the question differently the second or third time, or you will lose the inter-viewee's spontaneity.* "The freshness of a response comes right through the camera," says John Martin. "If you can see this person thinking, and you feel that they are arriving at these words as they say them, that comes directly through the screen."

The advantage of a taped field interview, of course, is that you can do retakes. You also have time to pick out the best segments. You can rewrite and reedit. Susan Stamberg said her average tape ratio was five to one. She usually taped 15 minutes of an interview to find three minutes to put on the air.

In a live field interview, however, the editing takes place in front of the audience. A live interviewer in a breaking news story faces some special hazards. You are particularly vulnerable to errors, rumors, libelous com-ments and your own emotions. When you or someone you interview says something in a live interview, there's no escape. Live is once only. Remember:

1. *Try to do your report in a location away from background noise.* Some noise is good for effect, but the background noise should not com-pete with your interview. Avoid a spot where onlookers can stand behind you and wave to their friends while you're doing your report.

2. *Attribute official comments to their official sources so that you are not reporting unattributed rumor.* If possible, interview a qualified official for comments rather than summarizing the situation yourself.

3. *Remember that most stations do not release the names of rape victims or of underage victims or suspects.* Victims' names in any crime—espe-cially in a live report—should be attributed to an official source.

4. *Avoid a "tease" that could inflame or increase the crowd.* Reports of fires and other tragedies often gather people to watch.

5. *Beware of hyperbolic verbs and nouns*—for example, cheated, gouged, perjured, scam, liar and villain.

6. *Avoid overstated, unconfirmed guesses about the number of people affected or the amount of property damage.*

7. *Double-check facts and statistics before you go on the air.*

8. *Take a deep breath.* You are the detached observer, not the involved participant. If you are wheezing anxiety, your audience will infer a holocaust from your statements, even if you're reporting a two-car freeway accident.

Using the Interview in Your Story

When you cut a taped interview, what do you look for? "That's easy," jokes Susan Stamberg. "You just throw out the bad quotes, and keep the good ones."

Use the same criteria to choose a broadcast quote that you would for a print story (see Chapter 9). A broadcast quote must be more succinct than the typical print quote, but otherwise they are similar. Write the story to use the quotes to their best advantage. Remember:

1. When you incorporate your interview into your live copy, you don't need to use quote marks.

2. Use attribution before, rather than after, the person says something. Otherwise your listener/viewer will not know who is talking until the person finishes.

3. Remember that broadcast quotes for on-air copy rarely run more than two sentences because your viewer cannot grasp more than two sentences at a time.

4. You can introduce a quote that you read verbatim by saying, "in her own words . . ." or "what he called . . ." to help your audience understand that you are quoting someone else's words. It is awkward, but sometimes necessary with an official statement, to say, "And today the governor said, quote . . ."

5. Be careful to use someone's exact words in your copy or in an interview if the quoted words could be at all libelous (see Chapter 11).

6. On television, to emphasize a quote from an official source that you don't have on tape, you can superimpose the words on the screen for impact. You also can use superimposed quotes if the sound is somehow garbled, but you want the audience to hear the person's

voice. Use this approach very selectively, however, because an audience can grasp only a sentence or two at a time. Whenever possible, your interview should stand by itself, unenhanced.

7. Read the copy aloud. Remember that the language for television is the spoken language. "If you read a paragraph in *The New York Times,* and you don't understand it, you can go back and read it again," says David Brinkley. "On the air, if the news person says something you don't understand, you can't go back and recapture it.

   "You can use more complex sentence structure on paper than you can in spoken English. When you are writing material to be spoken on the air, the best way to do it is to read it aloud as you write it. See if it can be said clearly, simply, directly. If it can't, then change it, rewrite it."

Interviews in the Studio

The benefit of a studio interview, both live and taped, is some preparation time. The interviewer is usually better briefed, either because the show has a producer or because the person often is scheduled a day or two before the actual interview, which gives the interviewer time for some research. Studio interviews are shorter when they appear as part of a daily news show. Longer, in-depth interviews are saved for public affairs and news interview programs.

A studio interview for a public affairs show can focus on a person who is one of a series of interviewees for a half-hour or an hour broadcast, or each guest can be one of three or four interviewees tied to a specific theme. A single guest rarely rates an entire show.

"Very few people will hold up for 30 minutes on the air," says David Brinkley. "It is not that a human being doesn't have enough to say to be interesting for 30 minutes. Most of them would be interesting for much longer than that.

"But on a particular point they are pursuing, what they know and what they're willing to tell, they're very seldom good for 30 minutes. It becomes repetitious. They come in with a few set thoughts in mind and the first 15 minutes they lay them on you. The second 15 minutes they lay them on you again."

In a studio interview, the choice of interviewee is crucial. "If the person has no interesting thoughts, no interesting information, or is unwilling to give you whatever thoughts or information he has, you're stuck," says

Brinkley. "You really can't do a good interview without a good interviewee." Try to review the people you select to be on the program.

Radio interviewer Gary Bannerman says he remembers a time early in his career when he was stuck with a less-than-interesting guest. "We had other people helping me decide what to put on the air," he says. "A guy on our staff who was obsessed with technical things thought this idea of moving thousands of tons of coal over mountains in a pipe was a fascinating topic. So I did a one-hour interview about moving solids by pipeline.

"The guest was a very distinguished engineer who had been all around the world. But he thought it was pretty odd that he was being interviewed, too, because he didn't think the topic was very interesting for a massive audience. I got 15 minutes into it, and I didn't have the good sense to bring it to an end. I just kept sinking lower and lower."

Interviewees who come into a studio have time to anticipate possible questions, so these people will be less spontaneous. Celebrities are so accustomed to being interviewed that you may have to fight to regain the microphone. Public figures sometimes want to give a speech rather than answer your questions.

"Every guest comes with a personal motive, and their personal motive is to promote—if they're politicians, themselves, if they're authors, their books, if they're businessmen, their job is to get air," says Bannerman. "My job is to subtract the promotional baloney from the reality."

Private people usually need more preparation to go on the air. "I don't expect someone who is not in public life to be able to spar the same way," says Ted Koppel. "I would never come at them in as tough a way. I would try very hard to do something or say something to put them at ease."

Gary Bannerman agrees. "Nervous people do not give good information, and most people, unless they are media hams naturally or have done lots of it, are pretty nervous when they come to a camera or microphone," he says. "The biggest job I have is to try to relax our guests."

Private people also have time to get nervous because they've told all their friends and relatives to tune in. "A funny thing often happens to private people," says Susan Stamberg. "We call a private person to set up an interview because we hope that person is typical. Sometimes people then become very aware of this responsibility. They become too well-informed, and they start getting guarded rather than just being natural."

So in a studio interview—live or taped—you want the guests and the format to seem relaxed and spontaneous, even though the program is planned and the interviewees are prepared. To encourage this spontaneity:

Before the Program

1. *Prepare the interviewee.* A person who is familiar with studio interviews needs less preparation than someone who is in a studio for the first time. "Someone in public life who is accustomed to interviews is going to leap at the opportunity to dominate the interview," says Ted Koppel. "It's very useful to deliver a kind of psychic punch to the solar plexus before you go on the air.

    "There was a senior state department official whom I told just before we went on the air that he was excruciatingly boring the last time he was on, and I hoped he had something more useful to say this time. Then boom! end of commercial, the program begins, and he's a little bit off balance."

    Koppel says he makes it a policy not to meet or talk with public officials before an interview because they may want some agreement about what they will discuss. "I don't want to put myself in the position where they're going to say, 'Ted, you understand I can't talk about such and such.' "

2. *Outline the program.* Although Koppel suggests you keep public officials off guard, an inexperienced interviewee needs some preparation. You can do this when you arrange the interview or in the studio before the program. Discuss generally what you will cover, without the specific questions.

3. *Names and titles are important.* You can make yourself look foolish and distress your guest before the interview even starts by mispronouncing the guest's name or by giving the guest the wrong title. Recheck this with the interviewee just to be sure.

4. *Stop a guest who starts to tell you a good anecdote before the show.* Many programs die in the preinterview. If someone has a story to tell, you want it fresh on the program. No matter how good a story is, it will be duller in the second telling than in the first.

5. *Advise the guests to keep their answers short.* This may not work, but at least you can try. Remind guests that a live interview works better when the questions and answers are succinct.

During the Program

1. *Pay attention to the interviewee.* You are a timekeeper as well as an interviewer, but don't let the timekeeping distract you from the interviewee. If the person is answering a question and you are shuffling papers, you will distract the interviewee. Focus on the

interviewee. Maintain eye contact, and be alert to the interviewee's answers. To help you summarize the interview at the end, keep a small notepad and pen to write down key points that you want to remember.

2. *Begin with easy questions.* You have time to ask preliminary questions before you probe sensitive subjects. Let the interviewee and your audience relax while you get accustomed to each other.

3. *Remember that succinct questions, delivered in a logical sequence, are essential.* Keep a keyword list of questions in case you need them. As in a telephone interview, remember your focus, but don't be afraid to take the interview somewhere new.

4. *Be conversational, but not too familiar.* Even if the interviewee is a personal friend, don't take unnecessary advantage of the friendship. The interviewee will be more relaxed, but people in the audience will feel offended by too many personal reminiscences that don't include them.

5. *Don't pretend.* "However limited the research you do, do some," says Ted Koppel. "But don't pretend you've read the book when you haven't, don't pretend that you understand the subject when you don't. No one ever looks dumber than when they act as though they have done the research.

   "An audience is infinitely patient with someone who says, 'You'll have to excuse me, but I really have not had time to read your book. From what I hear, it's a terrific book. Tell me, as you're telling the audience, why should I go out and spend $13.95?' If that's the best you can do, at least it's honest."

6. *Clarify on the spot.* Remember to give background when someone mentions a word or a concept that could be new to the audience. Ask the interviewee to define jargon or abbreviations. Avoid too many numbers because your audience can't digest them fast enough.

   "The broadcast media is the worst place in the world to start throwing statistics around," says Gary Bannerman, "because people are listening for essential truth. I can usually sidetrack an interviewee back into reality by saying, 'Nobody is sitting there with a pen and paper, taking your statistics. What is the point you're trying to make?'"

7. *Rephrase a rambling answer.* Ask the interviewee, "Are you saying that . . . ?" This gives the audience time to pause with you to understand an answer.

8. *Interrupt.* "The danger in live interviewing," says Sam Donaldson, "is the loquacious blabbermouth who just runs on, and you can't shut the person up. That's where you come out with a long interview, but very few different questions. You can interrupt blatantly by saying, 'On another subject . . .' Or you can let them down a little easier by saying, 'All right, Senator, we understand your views on that. It's quite clear. But what I want to know is . . .' Or you can say, 'Well, very good, but you're not answering the question. Let me repeat the question. . . .'" In a taped interview, you can select the important segments.

9. *Pursue difficult questions.* If someone says, "I don't want to comment on that," you have two choices—to accept that answer or to get them to talk. Rephrase the question. Say, for example, "Let me ask you again. Are you sure there's no politics in that? Not just a little bit?" or "Why don't you want to comment?" If someone is giving you yes-or-no answers, you can say, "Can you explain your thinking on that?" or "How did you reach that conclusion?"

10. *Use the immediacy to your benefit.* Someone who is on live can't turn back. You can trap someone who is evasive, or you can capture and expand on a spontaneous slip.

11. *Use silence.* Many broadcast interviewers fear the pause, but a pause can indicate that you have just asked a very good question that somebody can't answer easily. "To talk too much is a terrible mistake," says Gary Bannerman. "There are so many hosts that go on, and you hear a hundred of their words for every ten you hear from the guest. If you've got more to say than the guest, why do you have a guest there in the first place?"

12. *Don't be rude.* You are a stand-in for your audience. "Audiences have sympathies," says Ted Koppel. "They tend to empathize with the questioner, with the interviewer. They have certain questions that they would like to ask, and that they would like to have answered. But if they see you being rude, then all of a sudden they pull their soul out of you and transfer it to the interviewee. You've got to be very careful about how hard you push."

13. *If something goes wrong, acknowledge the problem.* "It's amazing how few interviewers take refuge in honesty," says Koppel. "They'll make up all kinds of elaborate stories to avoid saying, 'Something went wrong.' If something goes wrong, tell the audience. They see it, and on a live program, curiously, that is one of the things that

adds to the magic of watching a live program—the notion that something can go wrong. That's kind of exciting."

14. *Remember to conclude.* An audience wants a summary, a signal that you are finished. If you have kept notes, summarize your notes. If someone has told a particularly touching story, let that be the end. If you have to interrupt because of time, at least be gracious and quickly thank all of your guests before the program finishes.

A Final Word

What everyone hopes for in a live interview is a special moment, a time when the purpose of the interview seems clear and valuable. During a program about Amerasian children, born to American fathers and Asian mothers during and after the Vietnam War, Ted Koppel remembers such a moment on "Nightline."

"We had a young Thai-American woman on. She was about 20, and she had an American father and a Thai mother. In Asia, Amerasian children are really looked down upon, and she was talking about what it had been like growing up in Bangkok.

"She said that for many years, when she was outdoors, she never saw the sky. She always looked down. She was afraid to let her eyes meet anybody else's eyes because they might mock her or make fun of her.

"You could have heard a pin drop in the studio, and no one was going to interrupt that young woman. We just kind of stopped, and it was an extraordinary moment. When that happens, the only thing you can do is to just be grateful that it's happened, and let it continue.

"On television, you've got to remember that you're not only listening to words. There is also a camera there to show emotion. So if you see that someone is grappling with the moment, let it happen, let it evolve. Don't follow your format. Follow the moment."

John Martin
ABC News

John Martin graduated from San Diego State College (now San Diego State University). He worked for *The San Diego Union* and then in the Paris Bureau of *The New York Times*. He worked in local television news for eight years before he joined ABC in 1975. He is now a national correspondent for ABC, based in Washington, D.C.

John Martin has reported for ABC from 24 different countries, including Nicaragua, El Salvador, Great Britain, France, Poland, Israel, China and South Africa. This assignment took him to Brazil, to report on a unique underground operation that documented terrorism by the Brazilian military. Martin's description of how this story was put together shows how a television reporter must join interviews and pictures to convey a complete sense of emotion as well as information for the audience.

"I got a call from Lawrence Weschler, who had just written a book called *Americo Universe*. Obviously he's promoting his book, but the story was so compelling. He had heard it [the story] from Jaime Wright.

"Jaime Wright is a Presbyterian minister, the son of American missionary parents. His brother was active in the Catholic social worker movement and was ultimately captured and tortured to death. So, Jaime has made it something of a crusade to expose all this. I thought it was an incredible story, so I wrote a story proposal to Ted Koppel."

Martin proposed the story to "Nightline" on April 13, 1990. In that proposal, he wrote:

"In 1979, the Brazilian military government decreed an amnesty for all human rights violations by its own members. That set a small group of torture victims to thinking: how could they get even? They devised a secret, dangerous plan.

"The Brazilian military were technocrats: they kept records of their torture sessions. The victims figured a way to smuggle the files out of the archives and copy them overnight. A few dozen at a time, week after week for three years, the files were taken out, copied, and returned. The copies [were then] smuggled to São Paulo, hidden in convents and transferred to microfilm and computer, and indexed.

"They discovered, from the meticulous detail, that there were, for example, 275 types of torture; they found every address and location of every torture facility. . . . At the end of five years of compilation and study, they produced a 27-volume analysis of torture in Brazil, based solely on official records.

"But then what to do with it?

"The material was boiled down into a single volume. Cardinal Arns personally approached a publisher and signed a contract to produce the book secretly. On June 15, 1985, the book suddenly began appearing in bookstores all across Brazil. . . . Within a week or so, the book was a national best seller."

"Nightline" accepted the idea, so Martin left for Brazil on Saturday, April 21.

"The morning that we got there, we [shot tape] in São Paulo and [interviewed] the woman who had been tortured while she was pregnant and the Archbishop and then [went] off to Campinas and photographed the archives, which are imposing, impressive.

"The following morning we flew to Brasilia and met up with the Brazilian deputy. He drove us to the supreme military tribunal archive. It was Sunday and it was closed, so we did some stand-ups there. And I said, 'Well, show me where this office was [where the records were copied],' so he took me over to this building, which wasn't far from the archive. We shot that.

"Then we had a wonderful lunch at a lakeside restaurant near the presidential palace in Brasilia and talked more about the story. I interviewed him at the mall in Brasilia. It was a long interview, talking about his role in what they were doing.

"Then we flew back to São Paulo that night. The following morning we [interviewed] more victims. The principal one was a kid [Ivan Seixas] who had been 16 at the time he was arrested. We decided to [interview him] where he had been tortured, which was in the Sacindarma Prison. Then we sent Jaime with the crew to get a couple of exteriors.

"We did one more interview in São Paulo and that was Ricardo Kotschko, the journalist who had been recruited to write the book. Then we flew to Rio. That night we interviewed the colonel, whose daughter and son-in-law had been murdered, [along with] Cecilia Coimbro, one of the women [who had been examined by the prison doctor] at the colonel's house.

"The following morning I got in the van with the crew and took them to the doctor [who had examined Cecilia Coimbro]. This guy was really a facilitator of torture.

"That finished it. I left the following day. I came back and worked at home. I have a word processor that hooks up to the phone and I write into the computer and send stuff out. I got back on Thursday and I wrote Thursday and Friday. By Saturday, I had a script. On Monday, April 30, we [finished] it.

"It was one of the most ghastly stories I've ever covered, hearing what was done to the people. And it was one of the most satisfying to be able to put it together and have people experience and see it. I think it is really one of the most satisfying stories I've done."

NIGHTLINE
The Torture Book

Joao Luiz Moraes, former colonel	MORAES: "How would you feel if your daughter was beaten, tortured, abused sexually, and then killed in the vigor of her youth?"
Wife weeping at one side	MORAES: "And how would you feel if your son-in-law was tied to a jeep and dragged and forced . . . to inhale the exhaust fumes?"
Moraes speaking on camera	MORAES: "How would you feel if you knew that your fellow army officers had been responsible for the deaths of these two dear people?"
	Ja-woun Mor-ayes was a colonel in the Brazilian Army. His daughter and son-in-law were revolutionaries. The division in their family symbolizes the agony that was Brazil. Between 1964 and 1979 the military government kidnapped, tortured and murdered thousands of suspected subversives. For a time, the army was fighting armed Communist guerillas. Yet many of the suspects were students, workers, professionals and their relatives. The torture was used to get information and confessions.
Historical video: Sonia dead/alive	
Color shots: troops rushing	
Night surveillance photos, numbers *Color shots: people in custody*	

Blank screen: words in print	VOICE: "After being brutally undressed by policemen, I was made to sit in the dragon's chair, which is an electric chair of aluminum, with hands and feet tied and electric wires connected to my . . . tongue, ears, eyes, wrists, breasts, and genital organs."
1979 military junta	In 1979, the military government declared an amnesty for human rights violators. That meant no one would be punished.
Jaime Wright entering archive	But some of the victims and survivors decided to settle accounts with the torturers.
Ws Arns and Martin	They sent a representative to Paulo Cardinal Arns, the Catholic Archbishop of São Paulo.
Paulo Cardinal Arns, archbishop	ARNS: "He suggested to have a . . . history of what happened in Brazil . . . from documents, real documents, so that you could say . . . it is a history written by torturers."
Martin at court in Brasilia	MARTIN: "The records were on file in the Supreme Military Tribunal here in Brasilia. They were locked away underground in an archive: 707 cases involving more than 7,000 people. To get them, a tiny group of lawyers and victims set up a secret network."
Luiz Carlos Seixas, Brazilian deputy	SEIXAS: "First we rented a room; we leased two of the newest copying machines, hired two completely trustworthy workers . . ."
Seixas walking outside Congress	Luiz Carlos Seixas was a young lawyer who had defended some of the prisoners.
Luiz Carlos Seixas, federal legislator *Tilt from bench/people to building Seixas/Martin enter/exit elevator/hall standing outside door of office*	SEIXAS: "I went to the Supreme Military Court with the excuse that I had to deal with . . . some of these cases. I would then take these cases to the copying place, where . . . they worked as much as 12 hours each day."

Lawrence Weschler, author	**WESCHLER:** "They were absolutely sure, certain they were going to get caught. There was no way this could go on for long . . . to their astonishment, years passed; five years! They didn't get caught. At the end of this period, at one, one day, they suddenly realized they had done a million Xerox pages."
Brasilia skyline *São Paulo skyline, streets* *Cu people on phones, typing, etc*	The copies were smuggled from Brasilia to São Paulo, hidden in various locations, then transferred to computer tape for analysis, and to microfilm. Two newspaper reporters were hired to write a book. One was Ricardo Kotschko. His parents had come from Poland to escape repression.
Ricardo Kotschko, São Paulo journalist	**KOTSCHKO:** "What we are trying to do and what these people must do in Eastern Europe is to open up history in order that it might be rewritten. So society might be informed about what went on."
São Paulo skyline *Book cover*	In 1985, after 6 years of work, the Archdiocese of São Paulo quietly published the book. Military officials considered trying to stop it but gave up.
Bookstore display *Cu title* *People browsing, buying books*	"Brazil: Nunca Mais, Brazil: Never Again" became the best selling nonfiction book in Brazilian history: 225,000 copies in 23 editions.
Archivist opening file at Campinas	Today the documents are housed in this special university archive outside São Paulo:
Night: workers at tables from outside text with items	They catalogue the number of places where people were tortured: 242; the types of torture: 283; the names of the torturers: 444; the names of torture victims: 1,843, and the names of those who died or vanished: 269. And hundreds of personal stories.

For the victims, the book offers some vindication; for the torturers, shame. For other Brazilians, revelation.

VOICE: "Ivan Seixas was arrested at the age of 16 with his father. They were tortured in adjacent cells. Ivan heard his father's screams. His father died from the torture. Ivan was imprisoned in mental hospitals."

Ivan Ackselrud Seixas, torture victim

SEIXAS: "I remained in prison for 6 years so I knew what was going on. But when I finally left prison, I discovered people my age did not know, because of the harsh censorship . . . they accepted fear as the normal common thing. Today, when we see things happening in other parts of the world, I feel that the publication of Brazil Nunca Mais is very important . . . to show the mood that produces dictatorship."

Lobo walking

Dr. Amilcar Lobo is listed in the book as one of the torturers, which he denies, insisting he helped prisoners.

VOICE: "When I was taken to the prison, the first person I saw was Dr. Lobo. He examined me. He was present during the torture of two of my friends."

Amilcar Lobo, expelled physician

LOBO: "I participated involuntarily and as a doctor. I could never be in agreement with torture."

MARTIN: "You did not say 'No, I will not help?' "

Lobo speaking

LOBO: "I was intimidated . . . I never tortured anybody. I never touched anyone. The most I did was to listen to heartbeats and take their blood pressure and pulse."

Lobo denies any complicity, but even 15 years after his service ended, he remains haunted by what happened.

Lobo weeping	VOICE OF LOBO: "It is very important to publish about torture . . . it is time humanity realizes that torture must not be used."
Cecilia writing in office	Cecilia Coimbro was one of Doctor Lobo's 'patients'. She is writing a dissertation about the abuse of medicine by the military regime.
Blank screen: words in print	VOICE: "They took all my clothes off. They put a hood on my head and started giving electric shocks. They put water on the floor to worsen the effect of the electricity. They shocked my breasts, my stomach, and my vagina."
Cecilia Coimbro, psychologist	COIMBRO: "This is fundamental. History must not be forgotten. Once you remember history you stand a better chance that it will not repeat itself."
Moraes couple at square	Some survivors are building a monument on this square in Rio de Janeiro. Sonia Moraes' mother and father are seeking donations. They told young soccer players about the project.
Couple talking to soccer players	
Colonel showing kids diagram	MORAES: "We feel the monument truly represents a crying out against torture, a crying out against evil. And you'll be able to feel those emotions from the diagram."
Dissolve to model or sketch	The architect Oscar Niemeyer has designed a graceful, giant shaft that pierces the figure of a helpless human being.
Kids listening	MORAES: "It's a very beautiful monument, but torture is a very ugly thing. So it has to have a dramatic component so that people feel a revulsion against violence."

Moraeses in square or interview	**MORAES:** "Someone wrote in a letter: 'What will I tell my son when he asks: 'Daddy, what is this?' ' and the answer can only be: 'This is torture, my son. This is what happened during the dictatorship.' "
Cu figure on end of shaft	
Brazilians on streets	Now that other countries are ending dictatorships, they face the same question: punish or pardon. Perhaps the Brazilian example can suggest some answers. This is John Martin for *Nightline* in Rio de Janeiro.
Closeup of model	

9

How to Choose and Use Quotes

A quotation is unfiltered talk. The writer moves out of the way and says to the reader, "Here is my interviewee. Listen."

A quotation shows someone's thinking. You should use a direct quote only when it shows someone's thoughts better than you can—more characteristically, more succinctly, more authoritatively or more emphatically.

When you use quotes, you ask the reader to briefly listen in on your interview. Comments in quotations belong to the interviewee, not to the reporter. The reader hears the interviewee through the quotation without the reporter as an interpreter.

When to Use Direct Quotes

The people who talk in your stories should be worth hearing. Quotation marks bring attention to words. Because the words stand out, the quotations should be important to the reader. So you should be very selective about what you quote. Use direct quotations when:

1. *The quotation clusters words together in an unusual way.* Reporter Wayne Harada interviewed actor Pat Morita, star of "The Karate Kid." Morita plays a maintenance man who becomes surrogate father to a young boy who wants to learn karate. In the article, Morita talks about the importance of his first starring role in a movie.

"It's the mango on the tree that I thought would never grow. It's a plum, a gem, a fine, fine moment in my career, at a time when I really needed it to justify my existence."

2. *The quotation emphasizes or highlights a point.* Quotations can caputre a point or highlight a point of view that is important in a story. In "The New Puritans," Dinitia Smith of *New York Magazine* alternates quotes and description to explain a new fixation that Smith calls "deprivation chic." Smith says that many New Yorkers are like 41-year old Preston Handy, who devotes himself to his body every day.

For breakfast, Handy will eat a banana, a pear, and an apple, plus some 35 vitamin pills and various herbal compounds and bee pollen—"It tastes kind of like a mouthful of dry sand," he says. Before going to work, Handy will swim two hours; at midday he will skip lunch to work out for 45 minutes on the Nautilus machines at his local gym; in the late afternoon, he will run six miles around Central Park. He will then come home to a dinner of a yam and a baked potato, pasta "with a minimal amount of sauce," vegetables, lecithin liquid—"It's like licking the underarm of a snake"—and a multivitamin, "to cover anything I've missed."

3. *The quotation gives a concise, telling anecdote.* In this story, by Maryln Schwartz, a socialite explains the clothing requirements for Houston socialite Jan Williams' birthday costume party. Each guest could spend a paltry $150 to buy an outfit dressy enough to wear to lunch, which Schwartz calls "sale-rack chic."

The friends of Houston socialite Jan Williams are still talking about the "absolutely unique" 35th birthday bash she gave last month. It was a costume party.

Arriving "in costume" meant that all 38 women invited to the luncheon had to dress in outfits costing less than $150.

"Some people thought we should have set the limit at $100 and really made it tough," explained Mrs. Williams via telephone. "But I was afraid if I did that, no one would have taken it seriously. If the limit was $100, a lot of them wouldn't even have tried."

As it turned out, Mrs. Williams said, all of her guests were real troupers.

"These are women who spend more than $150 on their shoes alone. They just didn't have suitable things in their closets, so they went out and shopped at places they'd never shopped before," she said. "They were so clever and original."

For instance, there was guest Lynn Sakowitz Wyatt. She's the Houston socialite who's frequently on the international best-dressed lists.

"You wouldn't believe how absolutely adorable she looked," said Mrs. Williams. "She had on a cotton skirt, a cotton blouse and a straw hat. It just shows what you can do if you have good taste. And she scrupulously stuck to the $150 limit. She was so conscientious that, when she was driving over, she realized she had to take off her stockings. You know how much stockings cost today. It would have put her right over the limit."

4. *The quotation causes your reader to immediately empathize and understand the speaker's dilemma.* This UPI story reported that a jury took 10 minutes to decide that a retired couple living on an $884 monthly pension had the right to evict their 43-year-old son, who was earning $27,000 a year as a computer programmer.

"I spoiled the hell out of him," his mother said. "It just took me awhile to realize he's nothing but a chiseler. . . .

"I hate to say this, but he doesn't exist," Mrs. Zarna said. "I've replaced him. I got a puppy."

5. *The quotation reveals someone's character in a way you could not.* In this story, about the death of Clarence Nash, who for 50 years was the voice of Donald Duck, the quote from Margaret Nash makes the story special:

Called "Ducky" by everyone but his wife, Margaret ("I call him honey 'cause I knew him before he was a duck"), Nash's first professional brush with the animal kingdom came as drayman for a team of milk company horses.

6. *The quotation displays authoritative expertise or opinion.* The exact words of a significant public person, such as the chief executive officer of a publicly owned business or the president of the United States, are important because they often reflect important policy decisions. Direct quotations from a document, such as court records or a congressional hearing, emphasize the authenticity of your research.

People also become quotable experts when they are eyewitnesses to an event or a tragedy or because they are living the situation you are trying to portray—such as a truck driver in a traffic tie-up in a snow storm.

Someone also can be an expert, qualified to state an opinion, because of professional credentials and perspective. Richard Buck of the *Seattle Times/Seattle Post Intelligencer* included the comments of a logging industry expert in his story about the implications of a bankruptcy petition filed by Mayr Brothers Logging company:

"We're in the midst of a shakeout that has just gotten going, and there's no reason not to think this is going to get out of hand quickly," said Louis Miller, vice president of the Murray Pacific Co., a 75-year-old log-exporting company in Tacoma.

"I expect to see more bankruptcies every day," said Miller, who also heads a committee of 40 timber companies seeking relief from disputed state and federal timber contracts.

7. *The quotation identifies or denies blame for a serious accusation.* This lead on Francis X. Clines' story for *The New York Times* denies White House responsibility. Clines uses what are called "orphan quotes" (see pp. 143–144), because the exact official words are essential.

The White House announced today that two Government investigations had found that there had been "no violation" of the law in the preparation of a Central Intelligence Agency manual for Nicaraguan guerrillas.

But the White House statement added that the two inquiries had concluded there may have been "lapses in judgment" requiring disciplinary action.

8. *The quotation is the best available comment on an important issue.* When you can't reach someone quickly or the person won't talk to you, you may be forced to quote another news source. Jonathan Alter of *Newsweek* used a quote in a story from another magazine to capture an important criticism of the press for his article, "The Media in the Dock."

Sometimes, of course, the press corps is just plain rude, as anyone who has emerged teeth intact from a stampede of camera crews can testify. Lenny Skutnick, a government clerk who became a one-minute media hero when he pulled a victim from the icy Potomac River after the 1982 Air Florida plane crash, was quoted in last month's *Washingtonian* magazine saying, "They [the press would] come over and just take over the place. They'd use our bathroom and help themselves to the coffee and use the phone."

9. *The quotation unravels the speaker's characteristic rhythm and cadence of language.* Writing for *The* (Jackson, Mississippi) *Clarion-Ledger,* Raad Cawthon told the story of John Holland, known as the "Old Skinman" because of the way he cooks fried pork skins.

The Old Skinman draws the line in the Southern culinary dirt and dares anyone to step over it.

"All the others cooks their artificial. Mine is supernatural."

Tough talk, but John Holland, otherwise known as the Old Skinman, can back it up. If you don't believe it, just wrap your lips around one of his fried pork skins and crunch.

Pork skins fried crisp and light. The connoisseur douses them with hot sauce, two big bottles of which rest on the glass counter top in the Skinman's ramshackle Farish Street shop. Pork skins, barbecued or regular, are as Southern as the sweat from B. B. King's blues-stoked brow. . . .

"Can't nobody make 'em like me," says Holland, grinning an almost toothless 84-year-old smile. "Nobody else got the touch. I can't give that touch away. Gotta keep that. That's what keeps me moving."

When to Paraphrase

You can use someone's information without quoting the person simply by summarizing what the person said or by paraphrasing. A paraphrase describes for the reader what someone said without direct quotations.

Always attribute information that is not your own and belongs to the person who says it. Attribute statistics to the person or the agency responsible for the information. You also should attribute information when:

- The person is an expert. ("The Treasury Secretary announced today . . .")
- The person makes an unusual claim. ("Sonny Wilmore said he saw three green cats climb aboard the spaceship in his backyard.")
- The person is identified specifically with an idea. (Einstein's theory of relativity)
- Someone makes a criminal charge or a personal attack. ("The sheriff said Moonjay has been charged with six murders in Wallaby County.")

Sometimes reporters who have doubts about a story, or who are too lazy to figure out what to say, quote too much from the people they interview. A good writer selectively uses quotes to enhance a story, not as a substitute for good writing.

It's easier and faster to quote someone else than to tell the story yourself. Too many quotations, like too many doughnuts, give your reader indigestion. You detract from the good quotes when you force your reader to read through the bad ones. You should always summarize or paraphrase when:

1. *You can make a statement or clarify a thought better than your interviewee.* In this example from *The New York Times*, the writer mistakenly uses a long direct quote to let a psychiatrist explain how working mothers should behave with their children (italics added for emphasis in this and the following examples):

   According to Dr. Samuel Ritvo, professor of psychiatry at Yale, it is important for a mother to put the emphasis on nurturing rather than on achieving. *"A child today can get the achieving model and the nurturing model from one person, which is very different from previous generations,"* says Dr. Ritvo. *"But it's important that the mother be a good nurturer first and foremost. In other words, if the mother is a good achiever, and not a very good nurturer, this has a much bigger impact on the child than if the mother is a good nurturer and not a very good achiever."*

   Without clarification from the writer, Ritvo offers the reader too much to understand too quickly. This quote should be paraphrased to explain Ritvo's theory, which is very clear to Ritvo but leaves the reader saying, "Huh?"

2. *You can verify the information from several different sources.* In this example from UPI, the writer uses a quote to repeat a statement that has already been made, just one sentence before, in the text:

   Versluis, a big, strong-looking man with white hair, *was to have retired Friday* after 38 years as a truck driver.
   "He was going to retire today," his daughter said.

3. *The speaker talks about generally known information in common language.* In this story from *The Sacramento Bee*, the reporter quotes the obvious—information that could be stated just as easily by the writer as by the interviewee. The subject is Joe Spano, one of the stars of TV's "Hill Street Blues":

   He transferred from what was then San Francisco State College to UC Berkeley as a premed major—*"My father's a doctor"*—but an acting class and student productions carried his ambitions from the operating theater to the legitimate stage.

4. *You have only "orphans" to use because you do not have an entire sentence that is quotable.* **The Washington Post** ran this story about improved tourist business in Washington, D.C. The writer uses *orphan*

quotes—quotes around words that are taken out of the complete sentence in which they were spoken. Generally, you should avoid orphans because they do not reflect a complete thought. If you must use an orphan quote in a lead, for example, later in the story use the complete, full quote from which the orphan originated. In this sentence in particular the orphan quotes are unnecessary:

About 51 percent of the Washington area's hotel business is *"business meetings,"* including conventions as well as small company gatherings, said Kenny of the visitors association. About 35 percent of the visitors travel to Washington on other business, including a *"substantial portion"* for government business. The remaining 14 percent come for *"pure tourism,"* he said.

5. *You are writing about statistics or dates.* A writer who quotes somebody else giving statistics from a report is too lazy to study the report. You also do not need an interviewee to tell your reader when something happened; you can do that yourself. Give the interviewee more important information to talk about than, for instance, when an art museum held its first show. That's exactly how this writer in *The Milwaukee Journal* used quotes (Russell Bowman is the chief curator of the Milwaukee Art Museum):

"Our first show, in 1975, basically, served as a review of significant artists in the state *back to 1959,* when the art museum's first building—the original Saarinen structure—was put up," Bowman recalled in an interview.
  (*Saarinen is Finnish architect Eero Saarinen who designed the original portion of the Memorial Center. He died in 1961.*)

By including the dates in the quote, the writer creates another problem—what to do with the interviewee's reference to Saarinen. The awkward solution was to use the parenthetical explanation of who Saarinen was. An easier solution would be to paraphrase all the information, which is not particularly noteworthy. The information also does not need to be connected for any reason to Bowman.

6. *What you are quoting is authoritative but unintelligible.* Be particularly wary of government reports, which use jargon as common language. When a report or a person speaks in jargon, don't quote the jargon. This Associated Press story, which appeared in the *Seattle Times/Seattle Post Intelligencer,* begins with a good explanation. Then the government gobbledygook moves in:

Thousands of small farms are operated for pleasure, not profit, by people who work in town or have incomes that have nothing to do with their farming operations, according to a recent Agriculture Department report.

"*Minifarm operators* depend heavily on *off-farm* or retirement income to supplement or finance their farming activities," the report said. "This is generally not reflected in *aggregate farm income* statistics and other indicators that are used to formulate policy. . . ."

"Off-farm" and "aggregate farm income" are unfamiliar terms to the general reader. And what is a "minifarm"? The writer should paraphrase this statement rather than quote directly and should explain any unfamiliar jargon.

A List of Checkpoints

Here are some actual examples from newspapers and magazines throughout the country to show you how to use and how *not* to use quotations.

1. *Complete sentences make the best quotations.* You give your reader some guarantee that you are portraying an entire thought when you quote a complete sentence. Any time you interject a word into a sentence in parentheses, or complete a sentence for your interviewee, the context of the quote becomes suspect.

   To be useful, a quote should be a complete thought. Do not use parentheses within a quote when the quote cannot stand alone without the parentheses. In this story, a divorced legislator comments on the effect of politics on legislative marriages:

   "Anybody that says this business adversely affected their marriage [is lying]. That's a copout," said Assemblyman Richard Floyd of Gardena.

   The essence of the sentence is the phrase in brackets. How is the reader to know that the speaker actually means what is in the brackets? Brackets are useful to clarify pronouns or to clear up grammar within a verbatim quotation, but using brackets to clarify the major point of this quote makes this a weak quote. The writer omitted Floyd's concluding words and substituted a clarifying phrase. Instead, the writer should paraphrase and attribute the statement to Floyd or include the word or words that the brackets clarify.

2. *Be sure that the major point of a sentence is entirely quotable.* In this story about the successor to Miss America after the original choice was forced to step down, the crucial word is not in quotes, leaving the reader to speculate that the writer misrepresented the quote (italics added here and in the following examples):

> Charles said she hopes the image of the beauty pageant has *not "been tarnished"* and said her goal in the next two months is to "make us all forget this incident."

The keyword in the first quote is *not,* which changes the entire meaning of the sentence. The writer writes *not;* Suzette Charles says "been tarnished." The way this is written, Charles could have said she hopes the image of the beauty pageant has "been tarnished." The reader wonders since the writer omits *not* from Charles' quote.

3. *Beware of the ambiguity of pronouns.* When you use general reference pronouns in a quote (such as *it* or *this* or *that*), you often dilute the quote and make the reader doubt whether the person quoted is actually addressing the writer's point. In this article about reciprocal banking, which would allow out-of-state banks to do business in Maryland, the culprit is *it:*

> Maryland bank officials, who believe some form of interstate bank-ing is inevitable, are worried about who will be let into the state and what the competition will do.
>   "*It's* extremely sticky," said John Steffey Sr., a real estate broker who was handed the task of heading a reciprocal banking commit-tee for the state Chamber of Commerce, to which all the warring banks belong.

What is "extremely sticky"? The writer should try to use a complete sentence from the interviewee, such as "Reciprocal banking is ex-tremely sticky" or "It's [reciprocal banking is] extremely sticky." The reader then has no doubt about the interviewee's comments. When a direct quote is weak or unclear, paraphrase the speaker's comments. Use strong quotes or no quotes.

4. *When you have an effective word to quote, do not use the word alone in the text before your speaker uses the word.* This is from a story about twins who discovered they had the same disease at the same time— headlined "Twins' Cancer 'Flabbergasts' Doctors":

> When Joe Robinson went to donate bone marrow to save the life of his twin brother who was suffering from Hodgkin's disease, "flab-

bergasted" doctors made a discovery that may save Joe's life—he has the same cancer. . . .

"I was flabbergasted," said Dr. Alexander Fife, a University of Washington medical professor and a member of the Fred Hutchinson Cancer Research Center.

The reader will not be flabbergasted by the third *flabbergasted.* Use surprising words sparingly.

5. *Do not add to the quote before you attribute the quote to someone.* When you add words between the quotation and the attribution, the reader does not know where the interviewee's comments end and the writer's comments begin. This story explains who chooses to live in the downtown area of a large city:

> "We've had a lot of trouble attracting the kind of people we want," *people besides the unmarried, Yuppie resident who can afford to move to an inner city, said architect David Mogavero.*

In this quote, did Mogavero characterize the people as "Yuppie" or did the writer? The writer inserted questionable clarification that is not specifically in Mogavero's words.

6. *Do not characterize the quote for the reader.* Always leave the reader to decide what the quote means. This is a story about one of 21 people killed by one gunman at a McDonald's restaurant in San Diego:

> "He never had a chance," his daughter said.
> Later, *in an interview, she said with dignity,* "A lot of people thought very highly of my father. Many people loved him very much."

This quote has two problems—"in an interview" and "she said with dignity." Do not use "in an interview" unless you feel your reader will not understand that the comments came from an interview. Here, the interview is obvious. Second, "she said with dignity" detracts from what is an obviously dignified comment from the daughter about her father. The writer should not intervene to tell the reader how to think about the quote.

7. *Do not attribute a quote to more than one person or to no one at all.* In this example, a horrifying quote is attributed only to "police" rather than to a particular officer. The impact would be greater if the source were specifically identified.

He sat at the top of the stairs, a .32-caliber pistol in his hand. His two little girls huddled in the bedroom behind him; police hovered on the front stoop.

"I'm going to end their lives and send them to hell," *police heard him scream* about his children. "I'm going to blow up this place."

In the next example, the quote is a cute pun, but the source is unidentified:

Long hours and sheer determination have paid off for a Garden City firm that began selling processed potatoes to area restaurants *"on a shoestring"* in 1979.

A Final Word

A quotation can laugh or whisper, argue or appease. A people's history rests in its language. A quotation shows someone's personal piece of history, and you are the historian. Be a responsible record keeper.

■■■■ A N I N T E R V I E W I N G C A S E S T U D Y

Beverly Creamer
The Honolulu Advertiser

Beverly Creamer graduated from the University of Hawaii and went to work for the *Honolulu Star-Bulletin* in 1970. She has worked at *The Honolulu Advertiser* as a feature editor and a reporter since 1976.

This example shows how an interviewer must always make notes on as many details about an interview as possible because you can never be sure which details will be important to help you write your story.

"I was already behind the eight ball on the Max[ine Hong] Kingston story because a close personal friend of hers and mine who is a feature writer for our competition, the *Star-Bulletin*, had asked Max a year earlier if she could have first break on her second book. So when I called to ask for an interview after the rave reviews hit, she told me she'd agreed to give Sue Yim, my competition, the first break, but I could interview her shortly afterwards. I agreed, and decided then and there my story simply had to be better because it would be second.

"I already knew her [Kingston] as I'd done a story after her first book [*The Woman Warrior*] was out and was such a hit. Anyway, the interview was held at her house, with Max curled up cross-legged on her living room sofa that was covered in a hippie style '60s bedspread. The cat wandered about, and partway through, her husband came home and joined the conversation.

"Here's one point. You need to remember little things like asking what the cat's name is, especially when your interviewee spends some time scratching its head. When she said it had none, I was dazzled. I can't really explain why. In fact, I don't really know what it means. It was such a Zen touch that it spoke about her entire personality to me.

"For someone who gets inspiration from dreams, as Max does, a cat with no name becomes an intriguing little detail. I guess that's how it landed in the lead.

"It [the story] took several days to write. I worked on it two days at the office, in between duties as editor of the feature section. I felt very distracted as I worked on it, and ended up being inspired at home the second night and sitting down at our clanking old Underwood typewriter with the faded ribbon that I have never learned to change, and going crazy. The story just flowed. I finally stopped around midnight, axed much of what I had written at work, rearranged things the next day on the computer, and had a much better story."

Maxine Kingston: A Time for Applause

By Beverly Creamer
Advertiser People Editor

The cat with no name has wedged himself along the window sill, squeezing tight against the screen and, as she talks, Maxine Hong Kingston reaches out absently to tickle his fur.

She is curled up childlike, feet tucked under her, on the living room couch, its age and condition covered by a bright orange and yellow flowered bedspread. Her hair is grayer than it was four years ago and she seems so tiny, more so than ever.

Four years ago, she could well have been a newly arrived aberration in the literary world, who hit it lucky with her first highly acclaimed book, "Woman Warrior"—Time magazine called it one of the 10 best of the decade and it won the National Book Critics' Circle Award—and would peak out, with nothing more to say.

But it was no aberration, no mistake. In a few weeks, Kingston's second book, "China Men," will be out across the country (it's already on Honolulu bookshelves) and early reviews hail it as as powerful as her first, with a hint of 'Bunyanesque' quality. It's an analysis Kingston finds appealing and accurate.

"When I was writing it, I was thinking of Bunyan, too" she says in her small, hoarse voice. "I was thinking, 'Boy, these people are folk heroes, mythic American heroes like Paul Bunyan. . . .'

"I feel in a way this book claims America for China men, saying this is our country, we are the pioneers here, we are the pilgrims.

"When they came to Hawaii, when there were Exclusion Acts, when they built the railroad—I'm trying to establish these important dates, like 1776 is an important date."

The book is a compilation of a hundred interwoven stories about the men who came to this country as laborers and fashioned mythic, pioneering lives for themselves in a land known as the "Gold Mountain" in Chinese mythology.

"It's about real people who talk story, about real people who make up stories about themselves and other people. And they exchange stories. It's like these real people have

minds that think fiction, and so it's got to be fiction and non-fiction," she says. . . .

Maxine has written the new book in simpler language than the first, so it won't get in the way of the story. She believes the complicated language of "Woman Warrior" was a flaw. "This time," she says, "I keep the writing so plain that people must concentrate on what's going on rather than on the writing.

"It starts when Chinese first come to this country in large numbers, about 1850, although there were a few always, even at the beginning of America." It takes the Chinese up to the present time. "Each era is embodied in a different hero."

They are heroes who are so believable, so real to her that she can imagine their language, their gestures, and understand every motive. "I feel close to all of them because I have to be inside each one. I can see them very clearly, sometimes more clearly than if I weren't writing about them. It's like looking at a real person and really seeing him—and seeing how an ordinary person is a mythic person.

"I think that's what love is, too, to see somebody so well that you understand his motivations. You understand him and that's the same as loving him.". . .

10

How to Write What People Say

First, close your notebook and turn off your tape recorder. Your story is not in your notebook or on the tape recorder; it is in your head.

"What really burns me off is when somebody comes back from a very important story and sits down, plugs a tape recorder in his ear and starts transcribing the tape instead of writing the story," says Fred Chafe. "The reporter has not come back from the interview with a clear understanding of what happened. If he did, he would start writing the story and then listen to the tape to make sure he got it right or to confirm it."

Beware of tape recorder and notebook journalism. Don't let your notes dictate your story. If the story was in your notes, you could just dump all the words from the notes and the quotes from the tape onto the paper and then go home. Tape recorder journalism leads to stories that quote too much, that don't allow the writer to write.

Write your story from what you know, what you understand, what you intuit, what you observe. Then check your notes and/or the tape to verify quotes and facts. Be selective about the quotes you use.

Frederick Kempe of *The Wall Street Journal* takes you somewhere you might never travel in this story about gourmet eating in Russia. Kempe doesn't use a quote until the seventh paragraph, where the quotes sum up the story's theme.

> MOSCOW—Gastronom No. 1 isn't your usual Communist grocery store.

Its pre-revolutionary hall has mirrored walls, a stained-glass window, 60-foot-high gilded ceilings, and chandeliers. Crowds give it the air of a baroque Grand Central Station.

The lure of the place has to do with the rare items for sale: fresh Brazilian coffee, ripening Nicaraguan bananas, Cuban rum, and a rich assortment of meats and cheeses. In the culinary desert of the Soviet Union, it is something of an oasis.

Gastronom No. 1 has a new director. The previous one, Yuri K. Sokolov, was executed in July for illegally selling still rare delicacies—like black caviar and wild boar—out the back door to certain special customers—Western businessmen, Communist Party big shots and such.

A firing squad might seem stiff punishment for a little pocket-lining. But shoppers shuffling through Gastronom No. 1 on a busy Friday evening and the staff in neatly pressed white uniforms shed no tears. One woman buying tomatoes to make Saturday night's soup thinks Mr. Sokolov got his just deserts.

"He needed to answer for it," declares Mira, an attractive 58-year-old doctor. "You can't allow corruption to live. It must be stopped." . . .

Description of specific detail and background for the reader are very important in the Kempe story. But sometimes a writer can give too many details and forget the people in the story. When Kristin Gilger was working as regional editor for the *St. Cloud Times* in Minnesota, one reporter provided a very good example of how *not* to write a story.

"I had an unfeeling reporter interested only in facts and figures, not interested in people," she says. "I sent him out on an interview with an old couple in their 80s who lived in a frame house in the middle of a rural area with no conveniences, no electricity. I wanted to know why they lived like this, why they ignored modern conveniences.

"The reporter came back with a story about how old they were, how long they had lived there, their kids' names and ages, how much wood he chopped each day, how many rooms the house had, where he had worked, when he retired, how long he had been retired. It was like a census report.

"He wrote this totally dull story about these people. The reporter with the facts and figures didn't have the story at all. The story was these people. So I asked him, 'Where are the people in the story?' I love stories that let people talk."

People move into your stories as soon as you let them talk. Effective quotations are selected pieces of a conversation that only the interviewee can give the reader. As a writer, you must deliver that quotation to the reader in its best form—with proper placement and economical yet responsible focus. You must also remember appropriate grammar, word usage and punctuation so that the reader understands the interviewee's spoken words the way they were meant to be written.

Where to Place Quotations

You can place quotations anywhere in a story, but a quotation is especially effective when you position it as an introduction, to make transitions, or as a conclusion.

An Opening Quotation

Dan Fisher of the *Los Angeles Times* used this quotation from the mother of one of 600 Israeli soldiers killed in Lebanon:

> JERUSALEM—"You go on a very thin border between being normal and being insane," said Raya Harnick. "And you never know when you'll tip either way. It's like heart disease—one day you feel a little better, one day worse. But you're always sick."

As a beginning the quotation immediately emphasizes the conflict's human consequences. The reader is listening in on a story told by the real victims of war—the survivors.

A Transitional Quotation

A quotation can carry the reader from one subject to another in a story. Writer David Remnick of *The Washington Post* uses quotations to make transitions and to conclude this article about the late Jacob Javits, who served 24 years in the U.S. Senate as a representative from New York. This story ran in the *Post* just before Javits died. Remnick carefully alternates description with quotations to help the reader complete this word picture:

> STONY BROOK, N.Y.—Jacob Koppel Javits sits in a wheelchair behind his old Senate desk, an 80-year-old public man.
> A form of Lou Gehrig's disease has left his body a husk. He cannot lift a hand to sign his name or greet a visitor. A stiff collar keeps his head from slumping onto his chest. A portable respirator pumps life through a hole in his throat and into his lungs. A nurse feeds him clear soup through a straw, a solicitous aide sets a piece of correspondence before him for his inspection and approval. . . .
> "I was an active man, strong and in close touch with the world. Illness, you never think of those things. You just go on for years,

working, taking life for granted, My illness is considered terminal. I had to think about what to do, what it means. And I decided I had to keep on as long as I could."

. . . Because of his illness, it takes Javits nearly three hours to prepare for the day, but what he does with the remaining hours is extraordinary.

He has given commencement addresses and testified before congressional committees. He is in regular contact with his colleagues and may soon write a book about his illness. . . .

"I had to take a boxing course when I was a student and the instructor told me to put up my hands. The next thing I knew I was on my behind. He told me, 'There, that's the first lesson. Hit them from where you are.' And that's what I'm doing. I'm sick. Maybe I won't live much longer, but I'm hitting 'em from where I am. I'm not giving up a thing."

A Concluding Quotation

A final quotation sums up, makes a circle for the reader that begins with the story's first sentence. A good concluding quote gives the reader a sense of wholeness. The last quote portrays everything in the story that precedes the quotation.

In "Perspicacious Wordsmiths Acuminate Panurgy in Scrabble," *New York Times* writer Michael Norman describes the Massapequa Word Players, a Scrabble club that meets every Wednesday in Massapequa, New York. One of the players is Dee Jackson, who tells Norman, "Shall we say I exchanged my passion for my husband for my passion for Scrabble?" Then, to conclude the story, Norman returns to Jackson for another look at her compulsion:

> "The highest score I ever had on one word was on 'jonquils.'" Mrs. Jackson said. "I hit two triple-word blocks for 356 points. I was playing against my son. He said, 'Nice play, Mom.' And he never played with me again."

Quotes Should Be Responsible, yet Economical

An interviewer can be tempted to become an avenging despot, highlighting any quote that makes an interviewee look foolish. Or an interviewer can act like a protective relative, working constantly to improve an interviewee's thoughts. A good reporter is neither. A good reporter must be a thoughtful caretaker of an interviewee's words.

During an interview, the conversation weaves in and out of a subject several times. The person says something at the beginning of the interview and then amplifies the point several times before the interview ends. Someone may shorten common words (" 'cuz" for "because"), add a few "ums" between words, or leave a sentence unfinished.

Your responsibility is to present a true, yet economical, version of someone's thoughts. To do this, you can combine sentences from early in the interview with sentences on the same subject that come later. You should remove the shortened words, and replace " 'cuz" with "because." Eliminate the "ums" and the sentence fragments. This is a courtesy to your interviewee, as well as to your readers.

Except when the interviewee's dialect is uniquely characteristic (see p. 141), punctuate the interviewee's comments so that they are complete sentences, and correct the grammar that differentiates the spoken language from the written. Be careful to maintain the person's style of language. Do not turn an informal *don't* to *do not* or *can't* to *cannot,* for example. You must be as true as possible to someone's exact words.

Unless you cite another source for your quote, your reader assumes you interviewed the person you quote. You make the reader too conscious of the interview when you say "in an interview with" or "in a talk with."

Be simultaneously faithful to your interviewee and to your story. If the interviewee's comments are unclear to you when you begin to write, review your notes until the interviewee's point is clear. Review the context of the quote—the sentences before and after the statement—to verify that the interviewee clearly means what was said. Review the question you asked, which helps clarify the answer. Before you write, ask yourself, "What does this person *really* mean?"

How to Spot Word Barriers

Each sentence in a good story steps unobtrusively forward until, after many graceful, crafted steps, the reader reaches the end. A reader will stop once, even twice, to clarify a mixed-up statement or an obscure reference. The third time the reader hesitates because of a misplaced quote, a misstated fact or an unclear anecdote, you lose the reader. Don't force your reader to take any backward steps.

Some of the barriers that cause readers the most trouble when reporters write what people say are names and titles, indefinite pronouns, homonyms, clichés and gobbledygook.

Names and Titles

The first rule of reporting, of course, is to always spell everyone's name correctly. Verify the spelling, even with common names like Carol Hanson and John Smith. If you don't check, you will learn too late that you interviewed Caryl Hansen and Jon Smyth.

Titles cause the same problem as names. Someone who has worked for 10 years to become an associate professor will be insulted if you use the title assistant professor, which is one step below associate. The National Organization for Women may write you a letter if you call it the National Organization of Women.

If you are writing a story about a couple, ask both people for their complete names. Some women retain their maiden name when they marry. Also, never overlook one partner so that later you have to write "his wife" or "her husband" because you forgot to ask for a name.

Another mistake reporters make, especially on a breaking news story, is to forget to get important names at all. When she was working at *The Davis* (California) *Enterprise*, Marlane Guelden overlooked the name of an unusual traffic accident victim.

"I recall going out on a deadline story about a horse that was caught in an overturned trailer off of Interstate 80. The horse owner was too upset to talk, and I was in a frantic hurry to call the story in over a pay phone—the first time I had dictated off the top of my head.

"I got the basics from the police officer but forgot to ask the name of the horse. The crime reporter who followed up on the story for the next day spent two hours calling the university vet hospital and everyone in town to find out the horse's name, so he wouldn't have to refer to it as 'it.' No luck." The next day, the competing newspaper printed the story, with a picture of the horse and a caption that included the horse's name.

The horse's name isn't crucial. But the story would have been more complete with the horse's name. Always remember to double-check someone's correct name and title. For public officials or businesspeople, ask for a business card. Names and titles always are potentially significant points in a story.

Indefinite Pronouns

Whenever you use *he, she, they, it, this* or *that,* make sure your reader knows which noun the pronoun represents. Consider these sentences:

> "Tina took her dog to the party in *her* costume at her friend's house," Karen said. "She said *it* itched a lot."

When the bus came, Alan and Frank lurched for the door, and then *he* said, "Why don't you go first?"

Grove said he was going to give up dating, vote in the city election, buy a new cat and shop for bean sprouts. *"That* should settle *it,"* he said.

Pronouns in quotes can easily mislead a reader, especially when the writer does not clarify the *that* or *this* or *it* with a parenthetical note. A gong should strike whenever a pronoun follows a series of clauses or names. Check the antecedent noun to make sure the meaning of your sentence is clear.

Homonyms

Most of us write by ear. When a word sounds right, we use it. Because we often write by ear, homonyms give us a lot of trouble when we quote what others say. Someone who is talking with you assumes you will spell the words in the conversation correctly. *Homonyms* are words that sound the same but are spelled and used differently. Review this list of common homonyms and their meanings.

affect	effect
capital	capitol
cite	site
complement	compliment
counsel	council
elicit	illicit
eminent	imminent
eyes	ayes
forth	fourth
hole	whole
it's	its
lead	led
lean	lien
pare	pair
patience	patients
peak	peek
pole	poll
predominant	predominate
principal	principle
scene	seen
some	sum

stationary	stationery
their	there
troop	troupe
weak	week
whose	who's

Clichés

Quoting a cliché is like telling a bad joke—twice. Tired writer + clichés = bored reader. *Clichés* are once-vivid phrases that have been used too many times. Reporters quote clichés when their deadlines are short or their minds weary.

One group of people who proliferate clichés are sports figures. They say the winning team *bombed, brutalized, smashed, creamed* or *destroyed* the opponent. Coaches are known to offer great wisdom, such as "It's a new ballgame now" or "There are no losers here. We're all winners."

But clichés can creep into any story where the reporter forgets to ask the interviewee, "What do you mean by that?" until the interviewee says something provocative and worthwhile. This list of clichés is just a beginning checklist guaranteed to put an instant glaze over your readers' eyes. Start your own list, and remember to keep asking questions whenever you get a cliché for an answer.

credibility gap
crystal clear
depths of depression
paved with opportunity
peace offering
point of no return
primrose path
rays of hope
reign of terror
right track
rousing victory
significant development
sign of the times
straight and narrow
tension mounts
unknown territory
unmitigated disaster
war clouds

"It may just be a sign of the times that interviewers in the depths of depression follow the straight and narrow to the point of no return instead of venturing into the unknown territory of clear thought," she said.

Gobbledygook

Government officials rarely speak with language dedicated to clarity. Bureaucratic language combines qualifiers, prepositional phrases and mystical rhetoric. Dedicated gobbledygook groupies adopt the motto "Use too many words to say too little."

Reporters who follow government often adopt in their stories the gobbledygook jargon of the people they cover. Do not quote gobbledygook. Kristin Gilger says that one of the reporters in her bureau came back with a story that said that the city would divide tax money by "councilmatic district."

Gilger had never heard the term, so she asked the reporter what it meant. The reporter didn't know. The reporter wrote "councilmatic district" because the officials said "councilmatic district." "I figure if I don't understand something, 80 percent of my readers won't either," says Gilger, "I got over long ago being afraid to be stupid."

Gilger asked the reporter to find out what the term meant before she wrote the story. What it meant was that each of the four fire districts would get money based on how many of the seven council districts each fire district served. A fire district that served two small council districts, for example, would get twice as much tax money as a fire district that served one council district.

This clarification took time—a phone call. The edited story was clearer because the reporter was forced to understand the information rather than just report it. Keep the following list of common gobbledygook phrases and their translations, and add any new ones you encounter. Remember to ask the always useful question "What do you mean by that?" until your interviewee gives a clear answer that is not gobbledygook.

Gobbledygook	*Translation*
along the lines of	like
at all times	always
at the time	then
at the present time	now
be in need of	need
due to the fact that	because
effect a reduction in	reduce

experience a growth	grow
give consideration to	consider
give assistance to	assist
give authorization for	authorize
in order to	to
in the amount of	for
in the course of	during
in the event that	if
it is our feeling that	we feel
it is our opinion that	we think
make application for	apply
make use of	use
make payment for	pay for
be able to	can
be unable to	cannot
on numerous occasions	often
prior to	before
take delivery of	receive
with reference to	about

How to Punctuate What People Say

A direct quotation in a story turns the spoken word into the written word. Correct punctuation and attribution ensure that your interviewee's comments will be read the way they were spoken.

1. *Use quotation marks to surround someone's exact words.*

   "I always eat a dozen eggs, a pound of bacon and 14 biscuits for breakfast, so I don't get hungry before lunch," said the 300-pound wrestler.

2. *Use a comma to introduce a quotation.*

   She said, "I was so tired that I put my toothpaste in the refrigerator."

3. *Put commas and periods that follow a quotation inside the quotation marks.*

   "I don't want to get married until I have enough money to buy my favorite car, a 1961 Edsel," she said.

4. *When you quote someone who quotes someone else, use double quotation marks first and then single quotation marks within the double quotation marks.*

"I told her not to go to the beach," he said, "but then she said to me, 'I'll go if I want to. You can't stop me.' "

5. *When you quote a person at the end of a paragraph, and that person continues to speak at the beginning of the next paragraph, do not close the quotation until the person stops speaking.*

University President Baxter Meriwhether says that most students today are working while they go to school. "Our students don't have as much time to go to football games and to join fraternities and sororities as I did when I was in college.

"Tuition is four times higher today than it was 10 years ago, and most of our students pay at least half the cost of their education. If I had to work as hard as today's students, I'm not sure I would ever graduate."

6. *Begin a new paragraph when a new person speaks.*

WRONG: "Sixteen years ago, I left this town for the big city and prayed I'd never come back," said Homer. "I wish your prayers had been answered," said Beulah.

RIGHT: "Sixteen years ago, I left this town for the big city and prayed I'd never come back," said Homer.

"I wish your prayers had been answered," said Beulah.

7. *Use brackets to insert a clarifying word or words within a quotation.*

"I don't think Homer should run for office again, even though he's been elected at least as often as any Republican in the state, living or dead," said Jesse. "He's kind of like your kid when he gets his first [driver's] license. You know he's old enough, but you don't want him to do it this year."

8. *If you omit a large section of quoted material from an official document or a book, you can use an ellipsis (. . .), provided the omission does not change the sense of the quote. If you have any doubt about the meaning of the statement, quote the entire statement.*

The report stated that the "United States government . . . would not be responsible for the actions of the rebels in Central America unless their actions support the stated public policy of the United States."

How to Attribute Quotations

1. *Use the all-purpose* said *or* says *to attribute a quotation to someone. Avoid judgmental words such as* revealed, asserted *or* clarified.

2. *In most cases, put the attribution after the quotation.*

"I'll never steal again," said Emily Stickyfingers.

3. *If one person talks immediately after another one in the same story, attribute the second person's comments before that person speaks. Otherwise, your reader will think the first person is still speaking in the second quote.*

WRONG: "I'll never steal again," said Emily Stickyfingers.

"I wish I'd never met Emily," said her companion, Gerald Quickwit.

RIGHT: "I'll never steal again," said Emily Stickyfingers.

Her companion, Gerald Quickwit, said, "I wish I'd never met Emily."

4. *When you quote two continuous sentences from the same person, the best place for the attribution is usually between the first and second sentences. Then you can omit attribution after the second sentence because your reader understands who is speaking. Do not add "she continued" or "he went on to say" after the second sentence.*

"I watched this little girl crawl under the barbed wire and through the bushes toward the statue of Lincoln," said the security guard. "Then she pulled some flowers out of her jacket, laid them across the statue's feet, and crawled out the same way she came."

5. *Use someone's title and complete name the first time you quote the person.*

"I am today announcing a $5 billion program to improve our public schools," said Governor Sharon Officeholder.

To attribute subsequent quotes, alternate a pronoun with the person's name or use the person's last name or title.

6. *In a long story, when you quote someone early and then quote several other people, remind your reader who the first person is (by title or a brief descriptive phrase) when you quote the first person again.*

"We arrested 50 suspects, and only one of them matched the witness' description," said Detective Seymour Coburn of the Middlebury Police Department. . . .

[Several paragraphs and quotations from several other people.] Detective Coburn said . . .

7. *Do not use facial expressions or physical gestures as attribution.*

"That's a pretty good trick," she winked.
"I just don't know what to do," he shrugged.

Dollars, Percents, Abbreviations and Parentheses

1. *Use a dollar sign to signify money inside a quotation.*

   WRONG: "I'll bet she spent 5,892 dollars to buy that boat."

   RIGHT: "I'll bet she spent $5,892 to buy that boat."

2. *When you use percentage in a quotation, write out the word percent.*

   WRONG: "I got a 10% raise," said Harriet.

   RIGHT: "I got a 10 percent raise," said Harriet.

3. *People do not speak in abbreviations, so don't put abbreviations within a quote.*

   WRONG: "I love Peoria, Ill.," she said.

   RIGHT: "I love Peoria, Illinois," she said.

4. *People do not speak in parentheses. If your speaker makes a parenthetical comment, use dashes or commas instead of parentheses.*

   WRONG: "I used to think that all (well, maybe not all, but at least most) men worry about getting bald," he said.

   RIGHT: "I used to think that all—well, maybe not all, but at least most—men worry about getting bald," he said.

Clarity, Conciseness, Completeness, Coherence— and a Cookie

Finally, review the entire story to make sure that what you have written is clear, concise, coherent and complete. Then there's that cookie.

Clarity and conciseness come from choosing the best words to tell the best story. Your second draft is rarely worse than your first. Remember to rewrite. But before you revise, leave the story where it is, and get away from your desk—even if only for 10 minutes. The longer you think about the story between the first draft and the second, the better your writing will be. "Complexity in language is simple," says David Brinkley. "Simplicity in language is difficult."

1. *Examine each verb.* Are most of your verbs active verbs? Or did you plod along with *is* and *was*?

2. *Examine each adverb.* Have you used an adverb to clarify a verb instead of looking for the best verb? "She moved slowly" can become "She crept." "He cried hard" can become "He sobbed."

3. *Examine each noun.* Look for the most accurate noun. "He is a very young boy" can become "He is a first-grader." "She made a lot of money when she was a young woman" can become "She made $25 million before she was 25."

4. *Examine each adjective.* Have you used too many adjectives or too few? Significant details make your subject memorable. What is different about this room, this person, this place that your reader should know? Remember that shades of difference color your writing. Is the room red or maroon? Is the person thin or stringy?

5. *Eliminate extra words.* Editors rarely ask you to make a story longer. Look for the villains of verbosity. Gobbledygook is easy to spot. So are qualifiers (*could, would, maybe, might, should*). But also watch out for repetitive redundancies (Did you catch that?) and words that guarantee windy sentences: *that, what, which, there is, there are, it is, it was, s/he was one who, back in (down in, up in, over in), is/are able, make, give* (see also p. 159).

ORIGINAL:	The governor's mansion, *which was built in 1880, is a building that* is historically important.
REVISION:	The 1880 governor's mansion is historically important.
ORIGINAL:	She said *that what* she is *able to do* is to take the train to visit her parents *up* in Alaska.
REVISION:	She said she will take the train to visit her parents in Alaska.
ORIGINAL:	Mildred *was a person who liked to* save money *when there was a* sale on a dress *which* she wanted.
REVISION:	Mildred saved money by shopping for the dress she wanted on sale.

6. *Favor simple sentences over complex and compound sentences.* Your reader is less likely to grasp a long, complex sentence than a short, simple sentence.

ORIGINAL: Marian wanted to drive her car to the store so she could buy a new hat, but instead she rammed her car into the front window of Bloomingdale's as she was turning the corner, but at least she was close to the store, so she left the car on the sidewalk because now she had a parking place, and then she went inside.

REVISION: Marian drove her car to Bloomingdale's to buy a new hat. When she turned the corner, she rammed her car into the front window. Now that she had a parking place, she left the car on the sidewalk and walked inside.

7. *Minimize statistics.* Don't ask your reader to grasp too much too quickly. When you need statistics, your reader may resist too many numbers bunched together. You also can use a chart or box to list statistics instead of writing all the statistics into the text of your story.

8. *Watch for regional language.* In Canada, candidates represent ridings instead of districts; in Louisiana, counties are called parishes. Clarify regionalisms for a story that will be published outside your area.

9. *Use a practical example or an anecdote to explain or personalize a complex point.* Often numbers are too abstract for your reader to understand without an example. Remember that numbers translate into money and people.

LEAD 1: The mayor today announced a new $100 million bond issue to subsidize low-cost, rent-controlled housing for the elderly on Front Street. The city subsidy means that the 540 new apartments will rent for $250 a month.

LEAD 2: The mayor today announced a new $100 million bond issue to subsidize 540 rent-controlled apartments for the elderly. For 75-year-old Sam Lockwood, this means he can move out of his $400-a-month apartment on Date Street into a new subsidized Front Street apartment that costs $250 a month.

10. *Whenever possible, write in the present tense.* The past tense makes your story less immediate, less interesting.

ORIGINAL: He remembered when the schoolhouse was one red building that sat in the middle of the field.

REVISION: He remembers a single red schoolhouse sitting in the middle of the field.

A story is *coherent and complete* when the reader feels that there are no gaps, no unanswered questions, no missing facts, no unnoticed details.

1. *Dedicate your story to one theme*—a single focus. Discard any tangential information. Create a complete circle of thought.

2. *Check every name, every fact, every detail for accuracy.* Delay a story rather than be inaccurate. Juxtapose statistics and facts—do they add up? Generalities are the first sign of a lazy reporter—"a number of people were killed," "millions of visitors in the past few years." Be specific.

3. *Check every story for fairness.* Have you included all points of view? Have you been true to your subject? Watch for words that overstate the story.

4. *Look for silky, unobtrusive transitions from one paragraph to the next.* Careful transitions create an invisible stitchery of structure. A reader who endures two "meanwhiles" is very diligent.

5. *Pace your sentences and your paragraphs for variety.* Alternate the subject-verb structure with surprising constructions. "He very seldom had any money" can become "Money is something he very seldom had."

6. *Remember how little you knew when you started.* Are you inside or outside the story? Be careful not to assume your reader knows as much as you do now that you're an expert.

A Final Word—The Cookie

Give your reader a reward for reading your story. First, captivate your reader—either by the quotes you use or by the way you tell the story. Then, offer a constantly surprising refrain that tickles the language and bewitches the reader.

Readers and viewers pay attention to a story for two reasons—information and entertainment. If the information is entertaining and the entertainment is informative, your reader will remember you and your story.

■■■■ **A WRITER'S CASE STUDY**

June Kronholz
The Wall Street Journal

June Kronholz graduated from Ohio University and then worked five years for *The Miami Herald*. In 1977, she went to work for *The Wall Street Journal*. She reported for *The Journal* in 36 countries, including India, South Africa, Zimbabwe, Zambia, Mozambique, Tanzania, Ghana, Nigeria, Pakistan, Sri Lanka, the People's Republic of China, Singapore and Hong Kong. In 1989, Kronholz left *The Journal*, and she is now living in Australia.

This example shows how Kronholz was able to use her observation and listening skills to create a very carefully crafted, well-written portrait of an African bus trip.

"I was traveling to Africa and India—places that Americans don't care anything about, and writing about subjects people don't want to know about—infant mortality rates, the success of foreign aid projects, and the availability of clean water.

"I had never been to Africa. I did a lot of tramping around the countryside. People were so astonished that a white woman would appear out of the bush.

"I had very limited access to government officials. The Africans are cautious about Americans. There is not that sort of tradition of talking to people easily.

"I knew the only way I could ever get anyone to read anything about Africa was to write the story so people would get captivated by the writing. People could get wrapped up in the tales—the travelogue and the color. Then I would slip in the facts.

"There are moments when I consider myself a good writer. Yet, when I hear people talk, I know that people can say things far more colorfully than I can write them. One reason you should never make up a story is because you don't need to.

"When I traveled on the bus through Africa, a woman on the bus was named Eyelid. The driver's name was Christmas. One bus was named the Shu-shine Express. Someone had a bathtub, and there were crates of beer on the roof. If I sat down at a typewriter, I couldn't invent things like that."

If You Want to Be Alone in Zimbabwe, Don't Take the Bus
You'll Find Almost Everyone and Everything on Board; Christmas Avoids Potholes

By June Kronholz
Staff Reporter of The Wall Street Journal

THE ROAD TO GUTU, Zimbabwe—The day is so hot that even the wild baboons have taken to shade, so bright that the land seems bleached of color. But Super Express Bus Service Ltd., picking its way around potholes on the dirt road between Fort Victoria and Gutu in southeastern Zimbabwe, has a full load.

Here on board are Eyelid Mutema and her father-in-law's chickens, Fred Sithole and the empties from his beer store, William Nyandoro and 660 pounds of turkey feed (the turkeys will make the trip next week), and old, blind Chief Mutema and his almost-as-old, almost-as-blind escort.

A bathtub, a plow, a set of bedsprings, two bicycles and a kitchen table are stacked on the roof. There's a guava tree in the aisle; sacks of flour and maize meal and sugar are stuffed beneath the hard seats. At every stop, odd-shaped bundles are heaved through the windows and odd-shaped women squeeze through the door.

Little Alternative

America's needs move by truck or train. But Africa's needs—at least, the needs of most Africans—move by bus. Few trucks are built in black Africa, and because of foreign-ex-

change shortages, few are imported. Trains are for the mining companies and run only to the sea. In Zimbabwe there aren't even many cars. Most people here are peasant farmers to whom a few stringy cattle represent vast wealth and an automobile is beyond the reach even of fantasy.

So that leaves the bus, and anyone who wants to travel, and anything that needs to be moved, piles on. . . .

At 9:30 a.m.—which is either departure time, 90 minutes past departure time or 30 minutes before departure time, depending on whom you ask—there are 54 of us in line. Small boys move down the queue hawking ice cream, bread leaves, plaid blankets, aluminum buckets and woolen ski caps.

An Adman's Dream

When the bus pulls into view, it is an adman's dream, painted on both sides, the tailgate and the hood with a giant advertisement for toothpaste. Beneath the windows is one word in huge letters: COLGATE. Above the windows is a promise: Helps Fight Tooth Decay. The bus is 12 years old and was burned out and rebuilt during the war. But it is dependable, says Christmas Mushoriwa, the driver: "No one has had to push in a long time."

Nursing mothers claim the seats in the back, folks with livestock tend toward the middle, young men dispute the seats in front. Christmas Mushoriwa locks himself in a steel-mesh cage he calls "the cockpit" and points the bus toward Gutu.

People travel in Africa for the same reasons they travel in America. William Nyandoro, a 46-year-old farmer, had something to buy in Fort Victoria: his turkey feed, a sack of sugar-bean seeds, a plow wheel and a plowshare. He can't buy these in Gutu and he can't sell his turkeys there; he'll bring them to town next week. From farm to market takes 10½ hours each way—"a long trip for a young man, a very long trip for an old one," he says.

Elria Shumba, 34 and also a farmer, had something to sell. He arrived in Fort Victoria last night, sold 198 pounds of peanuts door-to-door for $21, and now is going home for more.

Mary Mutema is on the way to her grandmother's house to show off her baby daughter, Beaut. Askilia Maposa has been visiting her husband, a migrant worker on a sugar plantation, and walked most of the night to reach the bus. Two young girls plan to visit their married sister. "Maybe she has husbands for us," one giggles. . . .

These buses, which look like U.S. school buses but aren't nearly as comfortable, are supposed to hold 78 passengers. We'll take on 88 today. It would have been even more, but the Super Express's rival, Shu-Shine Bus Co., bumped down the road

ahead of us, picking up a full complement. Shu-Shine doesn't have a return service tonight, however, so "we will be in great discomfort from the crowd," says Joseph Ndoro, who makes a weekly trip to the clinic in Gutu.

Zimbabwe has ordered a $150 fine for any bus caught overloading. But there are only eight highway patrol cars in the country, so the odds of being caught are as slim as the cattle hereabouts. The government also threatens to revoke the license of any bus caught belching too much smoke. "But 90% of the people depend totally on the bus," says Mr. Tsomondo. "How can we take it away from them?" In another safety measure, the government talked of prohibiting knitting on board, concluding that knitting needles were a hazard of the sharpest magnitude. Eventually it gave up on that idea. . . .

Outside Nerupiri, the bus stops for Fred Sithole, who heaves crate after crate of empty beer bottles onto the roof. No one hears them there over the din of protesting chickens, snuffling children and the good-natured ribbing of a man who is doing the unmanly: holding a baby in his lap.

Mr. Sithole makes three bus trips a week to provision his bottle store. Today he'll buy six crates of "clear" beer and 200 cartons of "opaque" beer, the thick, oatmeal-like sludge that's traditional in Africa. When the Super Express drops him off tonight, he'll load his goods onto an ox cart for the last five miles. Until bus service resumed last year, Mr. Sithole says, "I made the whole trip by ox cart. I was always tired. The ox was tired, too."

At 1:30 p.m., the Super Express reaches Gutu, a weary row of butcher shops and general stores that is the center of commerce for the tribal reserve. Mail is delivered to the post office, Mr. Ndoro is delivered to the clinic, Mr. Sithole is delivered to the liquor wholesaler.

There is some disagreement over whether we are late, early or on time, the confusion arising from uncertainty about when we were to have left Fort Victoria this morning. But Christmas Mushoriwa is adamant that the bus will leave again at 3.

"Maybe 3:30," he says upon consideration. He has been making the trip seven days a week since 1954 and earns $51.15 a week for his effort.

We have made the 51-mile dash in four hours today, but the return—over the swollen river in the gathering darkness—will take longer, Mr. Mushoriwa predicts. With two hours, maybe 2½ hours before departure, passengers already are camped in the bus.

I find Gutu's only taxi, negotiate a $54 fare back to Fort Victoria and share the back seat with an oil drum and a quantity of firewood.

11

What You Should Know About Legalities and Ethics

"**M**any people who make up juries don't like the news media," says attorney Bruce W. Sanford in his book, *Synopsis of the Law of Libel and the Right of Privacy*. "They think reporters are chronically careless with the facts and cavalier with people's reputations and private lives."[1] Sanford says the result of this public resentment is that juries are awarding higher damage amounts than ever before.

Before 1960, Sanford says, juries in libel cases rarely awarded more than $20,000. Today's juries have awarded $400,000 to a police chief for an article that reported that the chief was involved with illegal prostitution; $800,000 for a story that claimed that a husband and wife were divorced and the wife had been seen with Elvis Presley in Las Vegas; and $7 million for a report that characterized a motel owner as a drug dealer.[2]

The Libel Defense Research Center reports that the press loses 62 percent of the cases that go to trial, although 66 percent of those cases will be reversed on appeal.[3] The result is increasing cost for newspapers and broadcast stations to defend against these suits, even if the news organizations eventually win. It's not surprising that the legal and ethical issues of reporting are receiving more editorial scrutiny and discussion.

Most reporters have a general knowledge of how the law affects what they write and broadcast. Here is an overall review of some legal and ethical highlights for all reporters to consider.

The Laws of Libel

Libel laws are not uniform throughout the United States. Each state individually determines what is libelous, so only cases that are appealed beyond the state's jurisdiction reach the U.S. Supreme Court.

In 1964, the U.S. Supreme Court issued a seminal decision that affects the way the press uses the First Amendment today. A Montgomery, Alabama, civil rights group had placed an ad in *The New York Times,* accusing the police department of a "wave of terror" against black activists. L. B. Sullivan was the Commissioner of Public Affairs, responsible for the police department.

Sullivan sued *The Times* for libel. He had not been named in the ad, but he argued that the ad reflected badly on his department. An Alabama jury awarded Sullivan $500,000, and the Alabama Supreme Court upheld the award.

When the U.S. Supreme Court reversed the decision in New York Times Co. *v.* Sullivan, the court said that the press must be given more freedom to cover and criticize public officials than when the press writes about private people. The court said that public officials, unlike private citizens, must prove that a statement is made with " 'actual malice'—that is, with knowledge that it was false or with reckless disregard of whether it was false or not."[4]

Subsequent court decisions broadened the definition of public officials to include "public figures." The court then said that private citizens can become public citizens when they become involved in newsworthy events.

Since 1974, however, the court has begun to limit the definition of who is a public figure. The attorney who represented the family of someone shot by a Chicago policeman was not a public figure, said the court. Neither was a Michigan researcher who was criticized by Senator William Proxmire for using a $500,000 government grant to study monkeys under stress.[5]

This public figure determination is a key in defending a libel suit because when the court decides that someone is not a public figure according to the law, the person becomes a "private individual." A private individual does not have to prove actual malice by the reporter the way a public figure does. The private individual who is defamed must prove only that the publication acted negligently by not finding out whether what was published was false.

The Proof of Libel

To be libelous, a statement must be a "communication which exposes a person to hatred, ridicule, or contempt, lowers him in the esteem of his fellows, causes him to be shunned, or injures him in his business or calling."[6] Someone who sues for libel also must prove that:

1. *The statement was communicated to a third party.*

2. *People who read or saw the statement would be able to identify the person who was libeled*—even if the person is not specifically named.

3. *The statement caused actual injury that the libeled person can prove*— lost wages, humiliation, mental anguish or damage to the person's reputation.

4. *The newspaper or broadcast station is at fault.* Someone's status as a public official, a public figure, or a private individual determines just how much negligence the person must prove. A public official and a public figure must prove actual malice (see p. 172). A private individual must prove only that the press showed negligence (see p. 172) in gathering and publishing the information.

The Defenses for Libel

To successfully combat a charge of libel, the press can use three basic defenses:

1. *Truth.* Because a libelous statement must by definition be untrue, the best defense against libel is that the statement is true. The reporter, however, must be able to *prove* that the statement is true. Sometimes this means the court will ask the reporter to reveal confidential sources (see p. 174).

2. *Privilege.* This is based on the idea that sometimes the press must report information for the public good, that the public good outweighs the damage to the private individual, and that the story was believed to be true when it was reported. Privilege also covers libelous statements made by someone during judicial or legislative proceedings but reported accurately. Privilege for the participants in a legislative hearing is called "absolute privilege." Press protection for reporting these statements is called "qualified privilege."

3. *Fair comment*. An opinion cannot be proved true or false. The fair comment defense against libel covers the press' right to publish comment on public issues and to review, for example, restaurants, plays, books and movies. The opinion should be substantiated, however, and the attack should not be maliciously directed at one person.

A news organization that cannot prove that the libelous statement falls under any of these traditional protections is vulnerable. When a reporter makes a significant error, a retraction or correction does not protect the newspaper or the broadcast station from a libel suit. The retraction or correction may only reduce the amount of money the court will award if the libel suit is successful.

Reporters are surprised to learn that if their stories are questioned in court, reporters can be asked to name their sources and produce their notes and any records they used to write their story. In 1984, when General William Westmoreland sued CBS for libeling him in a television documentary, "The Uncounted Enemy," Westmoreland attempted to make his case by using not only the actual program but also the outtakes—taped segments—that were omitted from the broadcast. Westmoreland's attorney, Dan Burt, also acquired in pretrial discovery an internal CBS critique commissioned by CBS President Van Gordon Sauter that concluded that CBS was less than judicious in researching the charges against Westmoreland.[7]

A reporter who uses confidential, not-for-attribution information in a story becomes responsible for the unidentified source. Media attorney Sanford calls the issue of confidentiality of sources "the bloodiest terrain on the battlefield of libel litigation in recent years."[8]

Right of Privacy

The right of privacy is a 20th-century invention. In 1903, a New York court said that it was illegal to use someone's name or picture as an advertisement for commercial endorsement without the person's consent. This does not affect reporters. However, a reporter can invade someone's right to privacy by:

1. *Intrusion*. If you interfere with someone's privacy as an uninvited visitor, you are overstepping the law. You can photograph someone in a public place or at a public event, but if you photograph people inside their office or home, you must have their permission.

Reporters who use a tape recorder or camera without some-one's consent can come under this category (see Chapter 4); so do reporters who misrepresent themselves to gain entry somewhere or who trespass on private property.

If a reporter steals personal files because of their news value, the reporter can be prosecuted. If, however, someone steals the files and then gives them to the reporter, or volunteers confidential in-formation that is genuinely newsworthy, the courts will allow the information to be published.

One Washington reporter says that during Watergate one senior officer in the government "not only talked to me, but one night we went to his office. He had a private diary. He fed it into the copy machine and I collated it."

2. *Putting someone in a false light.* This interpretation can cover exag-gerations of the facts or thinly disguised biographies that can be identified with an actual person. Another risky situation is when pictures of people are juxtaposed with a caption or a voice-over that is defamatory because the people portrayed are not the people being characterized—a picture of a clearly identifiable woman walking down the street, for example, with copy that describes a rise in prostitution.

3. *Publishing embarrassing personal information.* The press can show two people walking arm-in-arm in a public place, or a worker at a major league baseball game when she should have been at work. The embarrassment is unintentional, and the acts took place in public. If, however, a reporter describes someone's private sexual activity or discloses potentially damaging medical informa-tion without the person's consent, the reporter is vulnerable. The reporter has stepped out of the role of journalist to become a gossip.

The Defenses for Invasion of Privacy

A reporter charged with invasion of privacy can offer three defenses:

1. *That the person consented to the invasion.* A reporter can claim that someone consented to an interview or gave written permission to be photographed.

2. *That the person is newsworthy.* A *public* person cannot charge invasion of privacy unless the person's name or picture was used for commercial purposes. A *private* person who becomes, willingly or unwillingly, part of a *public event* is considered newsworthy and exempt from protection for invasion of privacy. A reporter can also quote accurately from *court or other public records* about a private person. But a *private person whose private activities are disclosed to the public without permission* can successfully charge invasion of privacy.

3. *That the issue involved the public interest.* This defense is related to the defense for libel, that the public good outweighs the protection of the individual. In this case, the person who charges invasion of privacy also must prove that the reporter knowingly reported a falsehood or doubted the truth of the information when it was reported.

Anonymous Sources and Off-the-Record Information

Whether to use anonymous sources, or even to accept off-the-record information, is an ethical debate that can become a legal issue. Reporters who use confidential sources in a story for which they are sued face a double dilemma. They want to prove that their story is true, but they want to keep their promises to their sources. If a reporter will not reveal the source, the court may assume there is no source. The reporter then must independently prove that the information in the story is true, without naming the source, or risk losing the case.

Judges also can send a reporter to jail for disobeying an order from the court. In 1978, *New York Times* reporter Myron Farber refused to tell how he got information printed in *The Times* about 13 murders at a New Jersey Hospital. Prompted by Farber's articles, the state indicted Dr. Mario Jascalevich for murder and called Farber to testify at Jascalevich's trial. Farber spent 40 days in jail and the paper paid $286,000 in fines rather than tell how Farber got the information. The trial continued, with Farber in jail and without his information. When Jascalevich was acquitted, Farber was freed.

More than half the states in the United States have adopted *shield laws* to protect a reporter's right to keep private sources confidential. Some state shield laws grant *absolute protection*; others grant *qualified protection*. With qualified protection, the reporter is vulnerable when the reporter is the only one with the confidential information that the court wants. New Jersey had a qualified shield law when Farber was jailed. Make sure you understand the protections for reporters in your state.

Some reporters will listen only to information they can publish in one way or another—with or without attribution. Some reporters refuse to talk with an interviewee off the record. Some reporters say they wouldn't have anything to write if they didn't go off the record regularly.

Bill Nottingham says that when someone tries to go off the record, "they want to negotiate the use of the information. They want to tell you something, but they don't want to get caught for it." Nottingham says he's willing to negotiate, too. "I'll say, 'Wait a minute. If you're going to tell me who's buried in Grant's Tomb, we'll go off the record. But if you're going to tell me who's buried in your backyard, the answer is no.' "

Seymour Hersh, who covered Watergate for *The New York Times,* says, "If someone whom you trust and you know says, 'This is off the record,' you find the information elsewhere. You basically protect him. You don't have that many sources. If you have them, you keep them, and you make compromises."

Bill Endicott says reporters always must think about why someone wants to talk off the record. "Leaks are usually nothing more than somebody wanting to float an idea or a policy and see what happens. If they get a lot of static, then they can pull back."

Endicott says reporters who agree to go off the record face another risk. "Quite often somebody will want to preface something by saying it's off the record and then they tell you something you know already. So then you have that dilemma of convincing them that you knew it already. They're going to feel that somehow you have violated a confidence."

A reporter who goes off the record and then attributes the information to "a source close to" or "a high government official" may be faced by an editor who wants to know the source's identity before the story sees print. Doug Dowie says that when he was UPI Bureau Manager in Los Angeles, he wouldn't use a story on the Los Angeles wire that listed anonymous sources without knowing the reporter's sources. "The reporter could go over my head, but if they wouldn't share the sources with me, the story was not going on my wire."

San Francisco *Examiner* Managing Editor Frank McCulloch says he is flexible about sources' names, but he requires corroboration. "I am totally unwilling to foreclose news taken from confidential sources," he says. "But if a reporter won't identify that confidential source for me, at least the reporter must characterize the source. You must be able to come in with two corroborating sources or two corroborating pieces of evidence, or you have to guarantee to me that, if we are sued, the unidentified source will stand up in court and testify."

Because the interpretation of all these legal responsibilities varies from state to state, reporters and editors are understandably nervous. Bruce Sanford suggests 10 ways to avoid libel and invasion of privacy lawsuits:

1. Avoid slipshod, indifferent or careless reporting. Whenever a statement could injure someone's reputation, treat it like fire. The facts of a story should be confirmed and verified, as far as practicable, in accordance with customary professional procedures.

2. Truth is a defense, but there may be a vast difference between what's true and what can be proved to be true to a jury. When in doubt about whether a story is accurate, check it out. Remember, a retraction is not a defense to a libel action but serves merely to mitigate or lessen damages.

3. There is no such thing as a "false opinion," so you have greater leeway with expressions of opinion than with statements of fact. But base your comment or criticism on facts that are fully stated and accurate.

4. Watch out for the "routine" story of minor significance. It frequently doesn't get enough editorial attention and, probably for that reason, accounts for more libel cases than all of the investigative reporting and human interest stories combined. Make reports of arrests, investigations and other judicial or legislative proceedings and records precise and accurate.

5. Try to get "the other side of the story." A good reporter sticks to the facts and not to some bystander's opinion of what might be the truth if the facts were known.

6. Take particular care with quotations. The fact that a person is quoted accurately is not necessarily a defense to a libel action if the quoted statement contains false information about someone.

7. Never "railroad" a story through. Edit it carefully to make sure it says precisely what you want it to say. Don't use sly or cute innuendo to suggest some misbehavior that you don't describe explicitly. If you're going to attack someone or injure someone's reputation, do it right.

8. Avoid borderline cases of invasion of privacy since the law of the right of privacy is still developing. Egregious insensitivity to the

tender and non-newsworthy parts of a person's life may earn you only the wrath of a jury.

9. Don't use unauthorized names and pictures for advertising or other commercial purposes. Don't use unidentified pictures to illustrate social or other conditions when pictures of people who expressly consent, including professional models or staff members, will suffice and are readily obtainable.

10. If an error has been made, always handle demands for retractions that come from a lawyer for a potential plaintiff with the advice of legal counsel. A well-meaning but unnecessary or poorly worded correction may actually prejudice a publisher's or broadcaster's defenses in a subsequent lawsuit.[9]

Journalistic Ethics

Ethics is both an ancient and a contemporary debate. Aristotle was one of the first people to examine ethical issues, although he didn't write for a newspaper or host a television interview show. Reporters and editors are still working today to define what is right and what is fair in today's newsroom.

Attorneys know, for example, that it is unethical to commit a crime to advance a client's interest. Doctors know that it is never ethical to kill one human being to improve the health of another. Journalistic ethics are less clear.

Media attorney Joseph T. Francke says that ethical principles for journalists are "a system of policies in search of an ethic."

Francke says, "Before journalists can prescribe a system of ethics, they must answer some fundamental questions: What is the role of the press? Why is the press necessary as an institution? And what would the country be like without the press?"

Hoping to contribute his thoughts to the debate, commentator Andy Rooney offered suggestions for a half-serious Journalist's Code of Ethics:

- The word "journalist" is a little pompous and I will only use it on special occasions.

- I am a journalist because I believe that if all the world had all the facts about everything, it would be a better world.

- I understand that the facts and the truth are not always the same. It is my job to report the facts so that others can decide on the truth.

■ I will try to tell people what they ought to know and avoid telling them what they want to hear, except when the two coincide, which isn't often.

■ I will not do deliberate harm to any persons, except to the extent that the facts harm them and then I will not avoid the facts.

■ No gift, including kind words, will be accepted when it is offered for the purpose of influencing my report.

■ What I wish were the facts will not influence what investigation leads me to believe them to be.

■ I will be suspicious of every self-interested source of information.

■ My professional character will be superior to my private character.

■ I will not use my profession to help or espouse any cause, nor alter my report for the benefit of any cause, no matter how worthy that cause may appear to be.

■ I will not reveal the source of information given to me in confidence.

■ I will not drink at lunch.

"It needs work," Rooney said, "but it's a start on an oath for reporters and editors."[10]

Associations of journalists have joined the ethics exercise. The Radio Television News Directors Association calls their list a Code of Broadcast News Ethics; the American Society of Newspaper Editors has adopted a Statement of Principles; the Society of Professional Journalists, Sigma Delta Chi, has titled their guidelines a Code of Ethics; and the Public Relations Society of America uses a Code of Professional Standards.

Stanford communications professor John L. Hulteng says that journalistic codes of ethics can be summed up in these five principles:

■ Journalists must observe a responsibility to the public welfare; their impressive power should be employed for the general good, not for private advantage.

■ Journalists should provide a news report that is sincere, true and accurate; accounts should be thorough, balanced and complete.

■ Journalists must be impartial; they should function as the public's representatives, not as the mouthpieces of partisan groups or special interests.

■ Journalists must be fair; they must give space or air time to the several sides of a dispute; private rights should not be invaded; corrections of errors should be prompt and wholehearted.

■ Journalists should respect the canons of decency, insofar as those canons can be identified in a society with ever-changing values.[11]

Journalistic ethics are what scholars call "situational"—each circumstance is different, and each decision must adapt to that circumstance. Many readers never see the ethical debate behind a decision to publish or not to publish a story, or to hold a story for more research, or to use someone's name. Ethical debates occur in newsrooms every day. To be sensitive to the debate is to know that to ask the questions is just as important as to search for the answers.

SIX ETHICAL CASE STUDIES

Here you can test your own sense of journalistic ethics. These six case histories are about actual situations, as described by reporters who were interviewed for this book. Three situations involve a decision about whether to publish a story. The other three situations demonstrate how a reporter can shave agreements with a source to meet a story's needs and how a person can become involved in making a story happen. First, decide what you would do. Then see if you agree with each person's decision. The actual outcomes of each situation begin on page 184.

The Candidate

The reporter was writing about a local race for clerk of the court.

"I interviewed all of the four or five candidates for the race. One of the guys was someone you felt sorry for. He was an older guy, kind of a character.

"He had no chance at all to win the race. In the middle of the interview, he said something about his past being clouded. He trusted me by this point. I got the information out of him by saying, 'I am going to find out anyway.'

"He told me he had been indicted for embezzlement in another county where he had been clerk of the court. He had admitted what he had done and had made restitution. He had to resign. There had been a settlement, but he didn't serve any time. He didn't want me to use it, but he never said it was off the record. I talked to the people in the other county and got the correct records."

Should the newspaper run the story?

The Doctor

"This doctor had talked two women into doing breast enhancements by hollowing out their breasts and putting in silicone implants when they weren't needed. These weren't women who were looking to enhance their breasts for cosmetic reasons. He told each of these women that they had to have these operations. The wealth of medical opinion was that the operations were unnecessary. The women just lost the breasts altogether. They were just left with scars on their chests.

"He had a long history of drunken driving arrests and he had been in a hospital. He'd fallen down, he'd had brain damage, and he lost the use of part of his left side.

"I went to talk to him and he was kind of a pathetic guy in his late 50s. He swore that he'd been to AA, that he was no longer drinking and that all his problems had been cleared up. There were a couple of malpractice suits pending against him, but no recent judgments and no drunk driving arrests in three or four years. He said everything was better now.

"Clearly, there was a public health hazard there. He contended that was the past, that he'd gotten better. There was no way to prove that, one way or the other. I tried my best. There were a few factors that indicated he'd gotten better and a few factors that indicated he hadn't. There was no way to settle it.

"This guy, when he learned I was going to put it in the paper, went into a panic. He knew this was going to end his career. And I wrestled with this. I was using this guy to make a point."

Should the newspaper run the story?

The Celebrity and the Public Relations Person

The PR person's client, a national celebrity, was scheduled to fly into town the afternoon before his evening speech. The PR person had organized an afternoon press conference, but just as she was leaving to meet her client, the chauffeur who was picking up her client called her from the airport. "This guy is sick," the chauffeur said.

"I didn't want the chauffeur to bring my client to the hospital because of the possible publicity, so I told the chauffeur to take him to a doctor who is also my client," she says. "It turned out that the celebrity was in a severe depression. He had been experiencing a number of hardships, but he had decided to suddenly stop taking his antidepressant medicine. He didn't want the press to know anything about this, and he divulged all of this to me. Yet I knew that we had 20 people waiting for us at the press conference."

How should the public relations person handle the situation?

The Child Molester

This story concerns a man who was posing as a Boy Scout master and a Big Brother. The police told the reporter about this man, who had been molesting Boy Scouts and Little Brothers. He had been sentenced to two weeks in jail and then released.

"I decided to make this a larger story about how some child molesters tend to sometimes join youth groups to get access to children. Soon it came time to call this guy and get his side of the story.

"I called his lawyer. The lawyer first threatened to sue. I pointed out that it was public record and he said, 'You'll ruin this guy. You'll ruin his life,' and that was true. I said, 'I'm sorry. I'm going to print it.' The guy himself called up and he was tearful."

Can you guess the outcome?

The Secret Documents

"Sometimes I think some of what we do is sleight of hand. One case I did, there was an attorney for a major defendant in a case. The attorney had some documents about secret, sensitive minutes of an executive [confidential] meeting.

"I said, 'Let me see them.' He said, 'No, I can't.' I said, 'Look, I promise I won't type any copies. Just let me see them.' And he said, 'All right.' And he gave me about 10 inches of secret documents and he put me in a room to read. There was nothing in there except a telephone."

What should the reporter do?

The Reverend and the Dancers

In this circumstance, the reporter wanted to get a story, with pictures, about a fundamentalist minister and his congregation who were regularly picketing a topless bar across the street from the church. The reporter, who worked for a news service, read about the story in the newspaper and wanted to re-create the situation, not only so that he would have a story but also so that he would have good pictures.

"This was a pretty interesting story. Seems that the church members, including women and children as young as five years old, had picketed the bar the afternoon before.

"I decided that this was a story that needed a first-hand look. I needed to go out on this one, with a photographer, of course.

"When I arrived, no pickets were there. I waited outside for, oh, two or three minutes, and then went inside the bar. I met a few folks, including the owner and some of the dancers, and started talking to them about the church pickets. I asked the owner if he knew where the church was. He said the church was right across the street.

"So I decided to go across the street to the church. Sure enough, inside there was a bunch of folks, singing and chanting, and the reverend was leading them like a cheerleader at a pep rally. There was a stack of placards on sticks near the back of the room."

What should the reporter do?

ANSWERS

The Candidate

"I called the guy back and told him I was going to do the story. 'I will try to write it as sensitively as I can.' The guy was a reformed alcoholic. The story appeared and he started drinking again. But I had an ethical commitment to the readers to tell them what kind of person was running for public office."

The Doctor

"I talked to the editor about it. The editor's judgment was that he would go with it. I went with it. The doctor stopped practicing the day the story ran. He closed his office, and the medical board revoked his license.

"It's a case where I was appointed to play God with this man's life. To a greater or lesser degree, all reporters have to do that at some point or another."

The Celebrity and the Public Relations Person

"We canceled the press conference. Then we acted like he was being taken straight to the airport after his speech, which he was able to give because the doctor had treated him. We told the reporters that he had an emergency back home. We sent a shadow limousine to the airport, but he stayed at my house overnight.

"It was hard for me because I pride myself on not misleading the press, but I avoided their questions. I had to lie to people that I have to do business with regularly. I gave the media the name and phone number of his press secretary back home, but of course I had told her not to give out any information.

"We never did tell the true story to anyone. If any media person had gotten ahold of this, it would have been quite a juicy story. I reacted out of personal concern rather than trying to gain brownie points with the media, and that's how I make my living."

The Child Molester

"I didn't have any real qualms about it. What he had done was wrong, and it was a public matter. This was something where the public truly needed to know how this kind of thing happened.

"That night, the guy killed himself, thinking the story was going to run the next day. [The paper] had decided not to run it after all. So we ended up writing an obituary instead.

"People asked me after that how I felt, whether I really felt awful. I didn't feel good, but I didn't feel that bad. The guy killed himself not because of what I was doing, but because of what he was doing."

The Secret Documents

"I picked up the phone and called our newspaper's recording room where you dictate stories. And I said, 'Put on the recording machine,' and I dictated it all into the phone.

"I never talked so fast. Then I went out and I handed [the papers] to him and said, 'Thank you. I took no notes.'"

The Reverend and the Dancers

"During one of the songs, the reverend took a break from his preaching, and I eased up front to talk to him. I explained to him who I was and why the man with the camera was following me.

"I asked if he and his followers were going to picket the bar again. He said that they were, but didn't indicate when. I asked when.

" 'When the spirit of the Lord moves us,' I recall the reverend saying.

" 'Reverend, I'm a reporter with a worldwide news service, but I've got a lot of other big stories to do, and I don't have much time this afternoon,' I said, putting a little extra emphasis on the worldwide part. 'Do you think the spirit will move you in about a half hour?'

"He said that he believed it would, and I moved on back across the street in front of the bar. Now, would you believe that the spirit moved the church folks in about 20 minutes instead of 30 minutes?

"So there I was, watching the picketing. Then I decided to go back in the bar to see how things were going in there. So I began talking to the dancers. I told several of them something like, 'Well, some of those folks outside may be pretty nice. Have you ever gone out to talk with them?' They said they hadn't, so I suggested that it might not be a bad idea to just go out and meet some of the church folks.

"And you know, five or six of the dancers went right out front and began talking with the picketers. The dancers didn't even put anything over their dancing costumes. The reverend even started reading the Bible to one of the dancers. Our photographer went crazy. As for me, I got a pretty good story."

Today, this reporter acknowledges that he was definitely too over-zealous.

A Final Word

"The tough calls are always those that balance precisely two totally conflicting social values," says Frank McCulloch, who authored *Drawing the Line*, a collection of discussions from 31 editors about ethical dilemmas.[12] "Sometimes the answer is going to fall on the side of the public. Sometimes the individual will have to be sacrificed if the public price is sufficient.

"The all-encompassing question, within which all others fall, is accuracy and fairness. If we proceed as reporters honestly, accurately, and fairly, there are no ethical questions left."

 **NOTES**

Chapter 3

1. John Ullmann and Steve Honeyman, eds., *The Reporter's Handbook* (New York: St. Martin's Press, 1983).

Chapter 11

1. Bruce W. Sanford, *Synopsis of the Law of Libel and the Right of Privacy*, 3d ed. (New York: World Almanac Publications, 1984), p. 1.
2. Ibid., p. 9.
3. Aric Press, "Westmoreland Takes on CBS," *Newsweek* 54, 17 (October 22, 1984): 61.
4. New York Times Co. *v.* Sullivan, 376 U.S. 254, 279–80, 84 S.Ct. 710 (1964).
5. Sanford, *Synopsis of the Law of Libel*, p. 9.
6. Harold Nelson and Dwight Teeter, *Mass Communications Law* (Mineola, N.Y.: Foundation Press, 1985), p. 44.
7. Press, "Westmoreland," p. 62.
8. Sanford, *Synopsis of the Law of Libel*, p. 25.
9. Ibid., pp. 4–5.
10. Andy Rooney, "The Journalist's Code of Ethics," in *Pieces of My Mind* (New York: Atheneum, 1984), pp. 59–60.
11. John Hulteng, *The Messenger's Motives*, 2d ed. (Englewood Cliffs, N.J.: Prentice-Hall, © 1985), p. 24.
12. Frank McCulloch, *Drawing the Line* (Washington, D.C.: American Society of Newspaper Editors Foundation, 1984).

■ BIBLIOGRAPHY

American Society of Newspaper Editors. *Free Press and Fair Trial.* Washington, D.C.: American Newspaper Publishers Association Foundation, 1981.

Baldassare, Mark and Katz, Cheryl. "Who Will Talk to Reporters? Biases in Survey Reinterviews." *Journalism Quarterly* 66, 4 (Winter 1989): 907–912.

Biagi, Shirley. *NewsTalk I: State-of-the-Art Conversations with Today's Print Journalists.* Belmont, Calif.: Wadsworth, 1987.

————. *Newstalk II: State-of-the-Art Conversations with Today's Broadcast Journalists.* Belmont, Calif.: Wadsworth, 1987.

California Newspaper Publishers Association. *Reporter's Handbook on Media Law.* Sacramento: California Newspaper Publishers Association, 1989.

Collins, Nancy. "The Smartest Man on TV." *New York* 17, 32 (August 13, 1984): 22–31.

Dibenedetto, William. "Bill Who? Please Hold the Line." *Journal of Commerce* 383, 27,158 (February 2, 1990): 8A.

Freeland, Dennis. "Better Interviewing." *The Writer* 99, 8 (August 1986): 14–16.

Garner, Alan. *Conversationally Speaking,* rev. ed. New York: McGraw-Hill, 1989.

Ginsburg, Alan R. "Secret Taping: A No-No for Nixon—But Okay for Reporters?" *Columbia Journalism Review* 23, 2 (July/August 1984): 16–19.

Greatbach, David. "A Turn-taking System for British News Interviews." *Language in Society* 17, 3 (September 1988): 401–430.

Griffith, Thomas. "Winging It on Television." *Time* 121, 11 (March 14, 1983): 71.

Guzda, M. K. "A Question of Ethics." *Editor & Publisher* 117, 14 (March 10, 1984): 18.

Henry, William A., III. "Just Bray It Again, Sam." *Time* 121, 15 (April 11, 1983): 78–79.

Hensley, Dennis E. "Getting Impossible-to-Get Interviews." *The Writer* 93, 6 (June 1980): 18–21.

Hulteng, John L. *The Messenger's Motives: Ethical Problems of the News Media,* 2d ed. Englewood Cliffs, N.J.: Prentice-Hall, 1985.

_____. *Playing It Straight: A Practical Discussion of the Ethical Principles of the American Society of Newspaper Editors.* Boston: The Globe Pequot Press, 1981.

Kessler, Lauren, and McDonald, Duncan. *When Words Collide: A Journalist's Guide to Grammar and Style,* 2d ed. Belmont, Calif.: Wadsworth, 1988.

Killenberg, George and Anderson, Rob. *Before the Story.* New York: St. Martin's Press, 1989.

Kraft, Scott. "Shop Talk at Thirty: On the Doorstep of Grief." *Editor & Publisher* 117, 40 (September 22, 1984): 48.

Landau, Jack C. "Media Law Today: Tape Record Important Interviews." *Editor & Publisher* 117, 3 (January 21, 1989): 22–23.

Lehrer, Adrienne. "Between Quotation Marks." *Journalism Quarterly* 66, 4 (Winter 1989): 902–906.

McCulloch, Frank, ed. *Drawing the Line: How 31 Editors Solved Their Toughest Ethical Dilemmas.* Washington, D.C.: American Society of Newspaper Editors Foundation, 1984.

Mencher, Melvin. *News Reporting and Writing,* 4th ed. Dubuque, Iowa: Wm. C. Brown Publishers, 1987.

Metzler, Ken. *Creative Interviewing,* 2d ed. Englewood Cliffs, N.J.: Prentice-Hall, 1989.

Meyer, Philip. *Editors, Publishers, and Newspaper Ethics.* Washington, D.C.: American Society of Newspaper Editors, 1983.

Miller, Larry. "How to Land Interviews with Busy and Famous People." *Writer's Digest* 67, 3 (March 1987): 26–29.

Murray, Donald. *Writing for Your Readers.* Boston: The Globe Pequot Press, 1983.

Nelson, Harold, and Teeter, Dwight. *Mass Communications Law,* 4th ed. Mineola, N.Y.: Foundation Press, 1985.

Newsom, Doug, and Wollert, James A. *Media Writing,* 2d ed. Belmont, Calif.: Wadsworth, 1988.

Patrick, Perry A. "The 'Perfect' Interview." *The Writer* 101, 12 (December 1988): 18–19.

Payne, Stanley L. *The Art of Asking Questions.* Princeton, N.J.: Princeton University Press, 1980.

Pember, Don R. *Mass Media Law,* 4th ed. Dubuque, Iowa: Wm. C. Brown Publishers, 1987.

Peretz, Martin. "Unreliable Sources." *The New Republic* 189, 40 (September 12, 1983): 20–22.

Porterfield, Kay Marie. "Phone Interviewing," *The Writer* 97, 4 (April 1984): 18–20.

Press, Aric. "Westmoreland Takes on CBS." *Newsweek* 54, 17 (October 22, 1984): 61.

Robertson, Nan. "Pulitzer Winner Discusses Interviewing." *Communication World* 10, 4 (April 1985): 12–14.

Rooney, Andy. "A Journalist's Code of Ethics." In *Pieces of My Mind.* New York: Atheneum, 1984.

Rose, Louis J. *How to Investigate Your Friends and Enemies*, rev. ed. St. Louis, Mo.: Albion Press, 1983.

Rubin, Rebecca B., Rubin, Alan M., and Piele, Linda. *Communication Research: Strategies and Sources*, 2nd ed. Belmont, Calif.: Wadsworth, 1989.

Sandler, Roberta. "How to Interview Celebrities and Experts." *The Writer* 101, 1 (January 1988): 18–20.

Sanford, Bruce W. *Synopsis of the Law of Libel and the Right of Privacy*, 3d ed. New York: World Almanac Publications, 1986.

Spikol, Art. "Before the Interview: There Are Two Words That Every Boy Scout Knows and Too Many Writers Forget." *Writer's Digest* 67, 9 (September 1987): 8–10

———. "For the Record." *Writer's Digest* 64, 9 (September 1984): 16.

———. "Me and Ms. Jones." *Writer's Digest* 86, 12 (December 1986): 16.

Stamberg, Susan. *Every Night at Five.* New York: Pantheon, 1982.

Stewart, Charles J., and Cash, William B., Jr. *Interviewing Principles and Practices*, 4th ed. Dubuque, Iowa: Kendall Hunt, 1988.

Zinsser, William. *On Writing Well*, 3d ed. New York: Harper & Row, 1988.

INDEX